TV ACTING

A Manual for Camera Performance

TV ACTING

A MANUAL FOR CAMERA PERFORMANCE

by

JAMES HINDMAN

LARRY KIRKMAN

ELIZABETH MONK

Illustrations by Jim Silks

COMMUNICATION ARTS BOOKS

HASTINGS HOUSE PUBLISHERS
New York 10016

Published simultaneously in Canada by
Saunders of Toronto, Ltd., Don Mills, Ontario

Library of Congress Cataloging in Publication Data

Hindman, James Thomas, 1942-   TV acting.

  (Communication arts books)
  Bibliography: p.
  Includes index.
  1. Acting for television.   I. Monk, Elizabeth,
joint author.   II. Kirkman, Larry, joint author.
III. Title.
PN1992.8.A3H5   791.45′028   79-13857
ISBN 0-8038-7184-8
ISBN 0-8038-7185-6 pbk.

Printed in the United States of America

CONTENTS

PREFACE

Several years ago, the three authors of this book got together to develop a TV acting program at The American University, Washington, D.C. James Hindman and Elizabeth Monk were initially theatre-trained and oriented; Larry Kirkman's professional background was in television production and direction. All three of us worked to bridge the gaps in our individual training and experience in order to evolve a program that would really deal with the special needs of the actor working for the TV camera. Our most immediate need was for a book, a manual for ourselves and our students, which would provide a TV orientation, a common working vocabulary, and a discussion of the major issues of camera acting. Nothing was then, nor is now (as of this writing) available that dealt comprehensively with TV acting.

After an incredible amount of trial and error, of necessary mistakes and exciting discoveries, we felt that we had developed a sound and systematic approach to TV performance—one that combines our individual expertise with our collective experience in teaching television acting to a variety of interested people: theatre students, TV directors, stage-oriented actors, neophyte media personalities, personnel and management people working with video, public figures and so on. This book is a summary of our experience together. We hope it will fill the gap, will help the transition to television that so many performers, directors, corporations, artists and institutions are making today.

A note about terms: we have used *performer* and *actor* interchangeably throughout the text. Our reason for this is that both *are* essentially the same on television. As discussed in Chapters 15 and 16, anyone on television plays a role—dramatic or otherwise. Weatherman to Sit-Com star, the preparation each goes through is similar, and the camera performance technique is identical. Different video formats have different performance requirements, but acting and performing on television are simply parts of the same experience.

Video, television and *TV* are often used interchangeably, although they have slightly different nuances in various contexts. "Video" may refer to the whole of television—including broadcast, tape, direct live image, and supermarket surveillance. Video is also used to refer to non-broadcast production, as distinct from TV and television. "Television" may refer to broadcast video work in any form, anything that uses the airwaves. "TV" usually refers to commercial broadcast television— what gets watched on the tube day and night by millions of people everywhere. In some places in the book, these distinctions have not been important, so all three terms have been used interchangeably.

We would like to acknowledge a number of people who helped to make this book possible. We particularly wish to thank our students at The American University, whose questions, patience, and willingness to learn with us stimulated us to write the book. We also wish to thank Peter Kirby and Paul Rusnak for their technical and professional expertise. Our colleagues Glenn Harndon and Michael Hamilton read the manuscript and made invaluable suggestions. Finally, we want to thank Gayle Gibbons and Shannon Daley, who gave their patience and support to the entire undertaking.

Washington, D.C.
March, 1979

INTRODUCTION:

WORKING ON TELEVISION

Television is our new performing art. TV is faces, human bodies, performers who need the skill to make effective screen images. This book is addressed to video with a complete commitment to its unlimited future. By and large, those who work in TV production are accomplished, competent professionals. The television performer can also be a skilled artist, trained in the exacting demands of a technically complex medium.

Good training for TV performance requires a real understanding of what television is, what it shares with, and how it differs from, film and theatre—the traditional touchstones of great acting. The accomplished TV actor must be sophisticated about TV: he or she must understand what lens selection does to a performance; know how to create amidst chaos; be able to speak fast and move slow; believe that the silliest dialogue can sound significant.

This book explores successful performance on TV. That includes, first of all, *tricks*—ways of doing things simply and correctly, based on the working situation. Second, *methodology*—systematic procedures for getting effective results every time, and under any circumstances. Third, *background*—a broad understanding of why and how things are done in TV production. Fourth, and most important, *integrity*—a commitment to honestly and personally saying what *you* intend to with your performance. This book stresses all four factors in TV acting and will give you a close, careful look at how each one works. The purpose is to help you become a skilled and committed performing artist in television.

WHO SHOULD READ THIS BOOK?

The actor in training who knows that TV is the wave of the future, that jobs are available to people who have the skills to work on-camera.

The person who must make an occasional television appearance, and who wants to be as comfortable as possible with the working process in TV.

The trained and experienced actor who wants to make the transition into television, who wants to make stage acting skills work on TV with a minimum of difficulty.

The actual or potential video person who wants to know how to work with actors, to understand what's actually involved in creating a performance for the TV camera.

Anyone interested in the range and possibilities of television, in the performer's special place and special working process in television performance.

American involvement in television is legendary. American viewers watch more TV than those of any other country in the world: in 1976, 70 million homes watched an average of 6 hours and 18 minutes a day. TV sets occupy 97 percent of U.S. homes and beg for our attention in store windows, schools, taverns and almost anywhere else—thanks to portables. Non-broadcast video is developing so rapidly that the upcoming uses of television can only be guessed at.

The future for actors in television is almost unlimited. Currently, commercial broadcast TV employs far more performers than the legitimate theatre or film industry put together. Public television is now funding more and more creative broadcast productions. The home viewing—consumer purchase—market (video disc and cassettes) has barely been tapped. Video production, which demands skilled, trained performers, is increasing at an astronomical rate.

An entire new job market for actors is also opening up in non-broadcast video. Schools, hospitals, public institutions and service-oriented businesses are making their own video programming. Progressively cheaper and easier-to-operate video equipment means that quality programs, with trained performers, can be made inexpensively to meet all kinds of needs. A survey showed that in 1977 alone, 45,000 programs, totaling over 15,000 hours, were made by 700 profit and non-profit corporations. By 1980 these figures are expected to triple. Much of this work uses dramatization, with actors, in order to train employees, explain things to clients and give information to patients, for example. Programming on video cable, which is about to reach the traditional 30 percent market saturation that attracts big advertising money, is opening up another entire working area for performers that will quickly exceed what is now available on commercial TV. TV is no longer ruled by the laws of scarcity.

The nature of television is changing, from a limited cast entertainment service largely controlled by the three networks, to an inexpensive, flexible medium which many groups and individuals are making use of for information, entertainment and art. TV is primarily a performance medium. More TV means more jobs for performers.

A colleague of the authors runs a small video production company that uses the advertising logo, "Sooner or Later Everybody will be on TV." It's true that more and more members of the community find themselves being interviewed; becoming part of a program made for their office, school or neighborhood; or working on a video project to document something. The great American fantasy of being on the screen is becoming a reality with video. Though part of the American dream, television is at the same time intimidating; the camera seems like a barrier, and the equipment is a somewhat threatening mystery to the uninitiated. What works, and why, in front of the camera is mainly a matter of observation and experience. This book is intended to bridge the gap between expectation and experience, to make the process of working on television more understandable, accessible and comfortable for the performer.

Most actors, if they have much training and experience, are oriented toward the traditional theatre. Training for TV work hasn't really been available until quite recently; some colleges and universities and a very few private studios are beginning to offer acting classes for television. The transition is not easy to make: what works on stage usually doesn't work on the TV camera. Television acting takes a special orientation, and the purpose of this book is to provide the interested reader with that orientation.

WHAT THIS BOOK IS AND IS NOT

What this book is not

A substitute for an acting class
A technical manual about television production
A book about how to direct television programs
A guaranteed way to get a job on TV

What this book is

A good introduction to the process of acting for television, including the range of performance work open to you, realistically adjusted to the usual studio and location working conditions. Along the way, this book will orient you to the technical realities of television as they affect the actor. The authors wish to give you a basic literacy and vocabulary for television, including terms and working methods that are fairly standard in broadcast and non-broadcast video practice. The book won't make you a video engineer, cameraman or director, but it should make you comfortable around a studio and around the equipment that controls TV performance.

This book is focused on the actor's situation in television. Most people working in video have a technical training and orientation. For them, the actor is the "talent," something to light, mike and shoot with a minimum of hassle and disruption. The process of making a performance—as the weatherman or as a character on a PBS drama showcase—is beyond their range of concerns. The actor is left alone to present a finished product, which is then adjusted to the needs of the production. This book will take the actor, and anyone interested in what the actor does, through a careful study of the performing process as it works on television.

Performing jobs are generally hard to come by. Personal connections, union memberships (especially AFTRA, the American Federation of Television and Radio Artists, and SAG, Screen Actors Guild), a good agent once you are established, being in the right place at the right time, sheer energy and a willingness to hustle are what get people jobs. This book is designed to help you get hired a *second* time, to help make you effective at what you need to do.

HOW TO USE THIS BOOK

This book is arranged according to several areas of information on TV acting. Some readers will want to read the book straight through, to follow the continuity of the material. Others may have specific questions and will want to consult the appropriate chapters. Listed below are some major performance questions and some specific ways to read this book for answers:

A. You're a threatre-trained actor who makes a professional living, and you want to expand into video work. You need to know a lot more about TV in order to make the transition. What can you pick up from this book that will make television acting easier to understand, less intimidating to try?

Part One is designed to explain the technical and the aesthetic qualities of television from the actor's standpoint. Chapters 10 through 12 deal with the actor's physical and vocal image as well as the realities of casting to type. The chapters in Part Three explain concretely the practical issues of "Working Production." This background, plus further reading here as you acquire TV experience, should help to smooth the transition.

B. You have been invited to participate in a locally produced interview show, and you are going to be on-camera for the first time. You are petrified about the studio and dread making a fool of yourself. How can you cover enough of the basics to be comfortable while you are there?

Start with Chapters 7 and 8, which introduce the layout and equipment of the TV studio as well as the jobs of the staff. Chapter 19 covers the basics of makeup and costume for TV, and Chapter 10 covers microphones and voice work. Chapter 9 on "Shooting" will explain blocking and camera work, which will affect you. If you have time, Part One will give you a solid orientation to television itself, seen from the eyes of the performer.

C. You have a good chance for a small part on a TV action show which is being shot on location in your area. You have some TV experience, but you have never done location work or specialized program formats like an action or police show. What should you read to get ready for an audition?

With some TV acting experience, you should skip the first two parts of this book and go right into the third, which deals with performance issues. Chapters 10, 11 and 12 cover your physical image, voice, and your type—good preparation for a casting call. Chapter 16 on "Genre Acting" will be particularly valuable in introducing the style of work in TV action shows. Chapter 9 covers remote taping issues, while Chapter 17, "Performing," introduces many of the pitfalls of on-camera acting under special conditions.

D. You're an actual or aspiring TV director/producer, and you need to understand how to work with actors. Your technical training and orientation don't really help in discussing issues like line readings, character objectives and personality images. You need a common vocabulary and some idea of how actors actually work. Besides taking an acting class, how can you understand performers better?

Chapters 4, 5 and 6 explain the basics of how actors work with the medium of television. Chapters 13 and 14 give the basic steps for developing a character and role in any kind of dramatic work. Chapter 17 explains the realities and problems in on-camera performance. These chapters will give you a perspective on the actor's job for television.

The actual organization of this book is indicated in the Contents. When you need information on a specific point, find the topic there and look it up. The Bibliography at the end of the book will give you sources for further reading in many areas discussed here.

Television is a new art. Broadcast TV as a medium in its own right is less than thirty years old. Ways of doing things are fairly conventionalized, but they change constantly as television evolves new technology, new uses, new audiences. This book is designed to give you an orientation to basic ways of doing things that have been, and will continue to be, standard for TV. Much more technical information is available on video equipment and broadcast technology should you wish to pursue these topics further, but in our experience, the performer is easily swamped with too much information. For this reason we have simplified and condensed in order to concentrate on what technical issues affect performance, and how. Certain equipment—such as microphones—is important to the performer, so it is dealt with extensively. Other topics—such as broadcast technology—are interesting but less central to performing, so they are presented in a general discussion.

Television is growing and changing in breathtaking ways. The performer is central to video and is an essential part of TV's burgeoning future. Any actor with a serious interest in the medium, coupled with a sense of craft and an openness to new ways of working, can participate in the growth of television as a performance medium. This book is intended to assist this process.

Part One

THE TELEVISION MEDIUM FROM THE ACTOR'S POINT OF VIEW

1

THEATRE, FILM AND TELEVISION: The Development of TV as a Performance Medium

Television is a late arrival as a performance medium. Because of TV's pattern of development, rooted in radio and deeply indebted to film and theatre, many styles of presentation and performance have found their way onto the TV screen during video's first thirty years. From this eclectic background several TV performance styles have developed, tied together by the inherent limitations and strengths of the medium.

Despite its newness, TV has a rich history and a clear pattern in its evolution. The purpose of this chapter is to orient the performer to TV, to outline the modes of TV production, and to uncover the roots of TV's performance styles in movies, stage and radio. Most actors and performers have practiced their crafts on the lecture platform or in the theatre. At the same time, they have watched TV or had it on in the background for at least 20,000 hours of their lives. Probably they have also loved movies and spent another 500 hours at movie theatres.

Our experiences with stage, film and TV—their weight in our culture, and how they are reflected in, and reflect in turn, daily life—create expectations about acting in the media. In fact, TV makes special but conflicting demands on actors and performers. Some of these are rooted in conventions tied to stage and film and some seem inherent in the television medium. This chapter will sketch the elementary distinctions between stage, movies and TV that should help readers clarify their own preconceptions about television performance. This discussion will provide a background for looking at the specific characteristics of TV explored in the remaining chapters of this section.

THEATRE, FILM AND TV

Performance on stage is generally based on a narrative, linear structure, limited by actual time and space, presented before a live audience who can interact in its creation. The late nineteenth-century theatre tradition, which prepared the way for film, presents sustained realistic scenes, which the audience watches through the "fourth wall" like a crowd of voyeurs.

Film frees the actor considerably from the limits of actual time and space, takes away the live audience, and increases the documentary quality of the "fourth wall" effect. In fact, by enlarging the actor on the screen, film eliminates the need for large gestures or broad details of expression. Without a need to reach the last row of an auditorium, the actor in film can behave much more realistically. (If anything, real life behavior must be reduced in size.) Although film performers can no longer interact with the audience, the film itself, shown in a darkened room, draws the viewer into the frame to show the audience what is normally unseeable. The camera, moreover, controls completely what the audience sees—just a hand, an arm or a face. The part can stand for the whole: the clenched fist expresses the taut body.

In the stage tradition, actors create scene by scene: for the film camera, actors usually create frame by frame, aware of the camera catching a close-up on one line and then pulling back to a group shot on the next. A total performance can be as brief as a glance upward or a simple turning away. Magnified on a large screen with excellent resolution, one shot of an actor's face can say a great deal wtihout dialogue, without action.

Film can also place actors in the broadest context of their environment. Actors work onstage in environments that are only suggested with limited scenery, indicated by a single room, or created by several sets that must be changed during scene or act breaks. Film can show the actual background of any story fluidly. The environment in film may easily be as important as the performers.

TV is not film, nor is it stage; nevertheless, TV has both theatre and film characteristics. As it has developed, TV is theatre in close-up. Like the stage, television emphasizes dialogue and the performer—the body, the face and sound. Television has no equivalent to the film scenes that linger over rooftops or take us leisurely down a road. TV, like film, however, has the power to show us the unseeable; yet, unlike film, TV has a relatively weak, poorly resolved visual image. Audio is necessary to fill out the TV story, telling the viewer where to look and what to look for. The large screen, the focused attention, the better resolution of film all mean that the viewer gets more information in one shot with more detail. Film makes a fuller use of environment, creating impressions of visual atmosphere that are lacking in the TV image.

The size of a performer's head on the TV screen is roughly equal to the size of the viewer's head. This match of scale between viewer and performer is reinforced by the nature of the viewing situation: the lit room, the competition of other visuals and dramas at home, the familiar surroundings, and the continuous flow of TV programming. These factors all help to de-mystify the screen, making the set part of the furniture and the show a part of the room. TV is forced to rely on its own methods of commanding our attention.

In contrast to the visual power of film, television holds its audience largely with audio. The viewer's ears cannot escape the sound, which calls attention to every development on the screen. The actor's voice and background noise of the location are used to jar the viewer back to the faces on the screen. Sound tells the story in video. In the TV that most of us know, the viewer doesn't have to work at understanding through visual attention. Without looking you can listen to the dialogue, the screeching cars, the laugh track and, if you know the formulas, imagine in your mind's eyes the simplified reactions of the actors.

Though commercial television may oversimplify the TV image, one basic premise that underlies good work for the video screen is in fact *simplification*. By its very nature, TV tries to do as much as other visual media, with less information and with a simpler image. The television actor trained in other media goes through a sometimes painful reorientation because less is more on TV. So many skills of the trade learned in theatre or film will not carry over to TV: TV requires a simplification of effect, and actors untrained for this media create fussy or wasted performances.

You control your TV performance by choosing ways to simplify it, to select exactly the right gesture or pause to bring life to the material and to your view of it. The pattern of this choices becomes a style, a defined way of doing things. Commercial TV has its own style, however; your performance style has to be adjusted to the realities of what is actually being shown on television, playing off the context and expectations of the viewers.

THE DEVELOPMENT OF A TV PERFORMANCE STYLE

TV working styles were developed in early live broadcasts: Milton Berle and the Broadway-based Playhouse series like Goodyear, Ford and Kraft that came out of New York; Dave Garroway and Kukla, Fran and Ollie from Chicago; the *Today* and *Tonight* shows, Edward R. Murrow, Oral Roberts, the McCarthy hearings; and other events, news, vaudeville, Broadway and the illustrated lecture. Film and theatre, nevertheless, have also had an enormous influence on the development of TV performance styles.

From the early fifties onward, film has played an important role in broadcast TV. The development of equipment to broadcast film was part of the initial television experimentation in the thirties, and film was immediately integrated into broadcast TV news reports. Videotape editing and portable recording units that are now in wide use were not even available or competitive with film costs and quality until the mid-seventies.

Starting with *Cheyenne* in 1955, virtually all TV action shows have been shot on film: *Bonanza, Perry Mason, Gunsmoke, The Untouchables*—all the way through the current Aaron Spelling and Quinn Martin productions. By 1957 there were over a hundred TV series filmed in Hollywood each season. At the same time, Hollywood found an outlet—on broadcast TV—for its thousands of warehoused film features.

Many of the films of the thirties and forties worked well on TV because they were adaptations of, or were based in, stage techniques that Hollywood began using as soon as sound filming became practicable in 1929. On the other hand, many action movies made use of sustained long shots and crowd scenes, and the effect of these was lost when shown on TV. Meeting the challenge to find other techniques and "effects," the producers of TV action series came up with formulas that they thought would be more suitable for the particular medium of television. Jack Webb in *Dragnet* introduced the quick wide establishing shot that cut to a close shot, eliminating the conventional medium shot widely used in film. This shooting formula is now used over and over again in all genres on commercial TV: the wide shot of a building, the zoom toward a window, the cut to the interior, and the focus on a character at a desk on the phone is a common example.

By the late fifties, the action show had developed several of its own formulas for TV. Crime, cops, combat or cowboys, the action show has a distinctive visual style that subordinates character and plot to the action itself. Like the sit-com (situation comedy) genre, the action genre involves a situation that must be unraveled within the narrow time limit of the program space allotted. There is neither time nor room to pay much attention to characters, ideas, language, discussion. Things must happen quickly; accordingly, the action genre relies on the paradox, the twist, the surprise. Flashy plot devices rush the story along without complex development.

Most of the one-shot, made-for-TV movies are part of the action genre, although they also borrow freely from the conventions of soap opera and sit-com shows. Such TV movies are long on plot, situation and action, while being predictably short on character. Because the characters and situation are not part of a continuing series, the actor is less locked into a repeatable, simplified pattern of performance.

IMMEDIACY AND LIVENESS

Much of TV's appeal relies on its status as a kind of comfortable old friend in the house. The familiar, continuing character underlies most TV performance. Action, news, sit-com, soap—all rely on viewers who feel they know a character or performer. Advertising spots also exploit this connection with continuing characters. Bert Lahr, who had a renowned career in vaudeville, in movies and on Broadway, was stunned by the "success" of his potato chip commercial. His recognition by the TV public was based on those few seconds alone, irrespective of the rest of his career. A recent study shows that 85 percent of the country has name recognition of "Price and Pride." These A & P characters/performers are swamped on the street by viewers who consider them easily approachable, like old friends.

TV performers do not have the distance and glamour of film "stars." This seeming familiarity of TV characters is rooted in the basic qualities of the TV image: the screen's size, TV's ubiquity and its capability for live transmission. When coupled with the fact that these performers have been in your home, television creates a closeness and familiarity that makes it part of the family circle. Television's "live" quality was recognized and exploited from the beginning of broadcast TV. One action show even broadcast live—a cowboy series, shot on an outdoor set in Philadelphia. It was called *Action in the Afternoon*. This particular production attempted to create the feeling of a live situation even working within the framework of location drama. Such efforts reflected that attraction of "liveness" as a highly desirable quality in itself on TV.

The appeal of "liveness" on TV is based in part on the viewing audience's interest in the technolgy that makes live broadcast possible. On the news, for example, TV equipment—the minicam, the portable video camera—is brought to the viewers' attention as much as the news item being covered by the camera. All shows that acknowledge the audience carefully plan shots that will include behind-the-scenes activity. The evening news has wide shots revealing the studio beyond the set. Anchor people sit in front of a bank of TV monitors that show shots coming up. The anchor person interviews someone in another city, whose face appears at his or her side on a TV screen. The director could use a simple cut back and forth between the anchor and the interviewee, but that would not draw attention to the medium itself.

As much as television features the performer, it also features itself as a part of the show. For example, Ernie Kovacs sat in the TV control room narrating his "skits" in a relaxed, conversational, at-home style, while demonstrating the live, playful manipulation of images and sound. Since the time when audiences watched Edward R. Murrow presenting the Pacific and Atlantic Oceans live side by side in a split screen, the process of live production, and of introducing the technology that makes it possible, has been an important part of TV's hold on its viewers.

TV's potential for direct communication—which makes it more like a telephone than a movie—made the immediacy and conversational quality of talk, game and news shows very attractive from the beginning. "This is live!" "This is happening right now!" "This is via satellite!" are exclamations revealing the special appeal that separates TV from film. It was in this context that *Lucy, Sergeant Bilko,* and the early sit-coms developed a method of using several film cameras to shoot in front of a live audience. This shooting technique gave the productions the flexibility of film editing, but with the feeling of a stage vaudeville show.

Situation comedy is probably the most enduring of the video programming genres, although its style is somewhat updated every season. The popularity of twenty-year-old reruns indicates the fundamental strength of the sit-com format. Both the old and the new programs command an impressive percentage of commercial broadcasting time. The themes, gag lines and comic devices of sit-com are as old as the classic Greek theatre, but the video sit-com format was perfected in radio. The sit-com formula is elastic; elements of it survive in the historical epics of Public Television, as well as in the design of thirty-second commercials and such cartoon series as *The Flintstones.*

"Liveness" is a quality that people have come to expect from the TV medium. It provides the viewing context of nearly all broadcast programs, since the qualities of a live show can also be imitated in pre-taped or filmed shows that are later edited. *Burns and Allen* was done live for two years and then went to film. After Lucy and Desi introduced the method of multi-camera filming with a live audience, comedy and drama shows that were actually broadcast live soon disappeared from the air. Film was more profitable, since it made reruns possible, as well as syndication and international distribution. Even one talk-game show, a genre that seems made for live TV, was filmed; its reruns have been both popular and profitable. *You Bet Your Life,* Groucho Marx's quiz and talk show, had the feel of a live event, but the density and depth of his wit and his rapport with the guests was carefully constructed through film editing. Today, however, TV's live quality is exploited most successfully by the restrained talk show guests who allow you to see them thinking—with hesitations, slips of the tongue and an intimate storytelling style that establishes the TV performer as a friend in your house.

DRAMA AND TELEVISION

TV is an information medium, and the actor constantly performs in the context of real pain, real accidents. The contrast between "real" events and fiction creates more subtle actors, and at the same time destroys the empathy the stage actor is able to build through an evening's performance. The television actor can only reach the audience through the camera, an intermediary agent that only shows selected parts and moments of the performer's work. Real rapport with the TV audience is an illusion; the process of creating a performance is tremendously limited by the medium. Dramatic material on television has had to develop a special style to accommodate what television does to the performer's work.

The various dramatic playhouse series that originated out of New York from 1948 through the mid-fifties were successful in dealing with TV's realities, and they attracted a wide audience. These hour-long and 90-minute live dramas dealt in close-up with ordinary characters and situations. *Marty*, the story of a Brooklyn butcher, was done on the Goodyear Television Playhouse in 1953, and the play is characteristic of these programs. The realism of simple conversations in long scenes, played in real time, worked in marked contrast to highly edited films on TV.

These dramas rehearsed for one week before they were broadcast live. The actors and cameras were carefully blocked, and the director switched back and forth as the cameras proceeded to the next shot on their list. This continuous exchange of shots naturally led to the use of simple formulas for composing shots and a relatively slow pace in cutting from frame to frame. The style of shooting live drama inevitably emphasized rooms, conversations, faces. In contrast, the made-for-television type of film series, the action show, exploited car and horse chases, violence and the use of unusual environments that were impossible to carry off in the theater or on the TV stage. This was the case at the beginning, but soon the creators of action programs were to learn the lessons of TV-theatre and to develop a size and scale of program design that lent itself to the small screen, and the small audience in the living room. Relatively low budgets and tight production schedules, as well as a formula approach to production, also caused these series to rely on the strong point of TV—the face.

COMMERCIALS AND SPOTS

Film has played, and still plays, an important role in TV advertisements. Until recently, only film could give the visual quality that advertisers demanded for air time, which cost as much as $100,000 for 30 seconds in 1977. A type of local live or taped-*simulated*-live TV advertising, usually car sales, has been shot for some time using large remote video vans on location. This style is an outgrowth of all early commercials done live in the studio, as well as the man-in-the-street or woman-in-the-street testimonials and live-video style product interviews shot in film. In the studio, video tape is also used to produce simple commercials, such as the blindfold test or the professional advice situation.

More recently, videotape has been used both to edit and to produce TV advertising on location. An immense investment in the production of TV advertisements for broadcast has introduced working techniques that are new to broadcasting. Ads are designed with "painterly" composed shots, very rapid editing, animation and live action, elaborately mixed sound tracks—all translated to the requirements of the TV image. Portable video is used in advertising production in a way that imitates film style; there are few performing differences for the actor, except for the advantage of instant replay on video tape.

Spots are attractive for actors since they form the bulk of broadcast work, are lucrative, get you known, and are one of the easier ways to begin a professional career in broadcast TV. The commercial is a special case in TV performance style; it is not really a genre of programming itself, since it draws from the conventions of all other genres. Creators of commercials and public service announcements, all called "spots," take freely from dramatized action formats, sit-com characterization, news announcer presentation—any style that might occur on conventional broadcast TV. In effect, each commercial is a small show that fits into the expected flow of commercial television, using its genres; if the viewer glances away for a second, he or she may not know that the show has been interrupted.

NEW PRODUCTION AND PERFORMANCE STYLES

The news has been the testing area for new TV technology because of its demands for an instantly usable product. The use of portable video for recording news stories on location has changed the style of news "actualities," news remote production reports. Portable video operators are shooting longer shots, using more real time; the overall use of location reports has increased at some stations by as much as 30 percent.

Laboratory processing makes film a slower product than video, which can be instantaneously replayed or transmitted by microwave. This use of "actualities" has been the grounds for developing portable videotape technology that is already being used on commercials and in some dramas. It is possible that the advent of portable location drama will create a style that mixes film flexibility with a videotape tendency toward the use of real time. The soap opera and the sit-com may well move out of the studio and go on location.

Clearly TV is in the process of changing the way things are done. Inherited stage and film techniques are giving way to the demands of a rapidly evolving video technology. The actor entering TV now will have to master both old and new production processes, which will continue to co-exist for some time.

ALTERNATIVES IN VIDEO

New video technology is also bringing changes to the non-broadcast markets. Educational, institutional, industrial and non-profit video has had its growth stunted by the domination of commercial models that non-broadcast TV simply does not have the budgetary means to imitate. Stuck for years in boring lecture and panel formats, non-broadcast video is now making a transition to location production and documentary reporting styles. Most important to actors, non-broadcast video is beginning to make extensive use of the dramatic format and style, requiring acted characters from its performers. Training tapes are made by major corporations to help employees learn new equipment and introduce new procedures. Information tapes dramatize situations for easier viewer comprehension; medical information pieces on topics such as high blood pressure or a diabetic regimen use performers as doctors and patients, acting out questions and answers.

This use of dramatized video, mixing vignettes with narration and graphics, is opening up new work areas for professional actors as well as interested but untrained performers.

SUMMARY

Television has undergone a complicated evolution. Born out of radio, copying and borrowing from film and the theatre, TV has only slowly developed its own special production and performance styles. Of necessity, the TV performer has had to be flexible, adapting to a changing technology with an enormous range of potential screen images. By understanding where television is coming from—and where it apparently is going—the actor can adjust his or her way of working to whatever the production situation demands.

The stage actor, by contrast, works under nearly luxurious conditions. Long rehearsals—where the actor is the center of attention—are only one of the advantages in a medium that is completely oriented to the details of the live performance. The stage actor may have to adjust slightly to lighting and set problems in the theatre, but the performance itself occupies most of the creative time and energy. The performer gets to create the performance in continuous sequence, in real time, with the support of a live audience.

Basically, performing for TV means working with whatever is there, adapting to the technology and time demands of a complicated and varied medium. The next five chapters of Part One are planned to present the basic nature of television from the actor's point of view, with an eye toward helping the actor understand TV as a performance medium.

2

MAKING AND MANIPULATING THE TV IMAGE:
Video and Audio

Film and TV share the characteristics of the screen. The camera reveals activities that would have no impact on the audience of a stage production. The close-up and the detail shot study everyday living and environment. The act of putting on socks or buttoning a coat can be seen so closely that the actor can use these gestures to say a great deal about the character and the story. Some images belong on the screen and would not survive a transfer to the stage. For example, there is the famous scene in which W.C. Fields laboriously puts on his socks and shoes as his wife pushes him out of bed to interrupt the burglars in the basement. The scene relies on body and facial detail, grimaces and mutterings his wife can't see, the slow work with his clothes and the intercutting with the burglars in the basement.

As two-dimensional media, TV and film share the common problem of trying to create a three-dimensional effect on a flat surface. Unlike a live theatre performance, where the audience can almost touch the actors, film and television are faced with the chore of drawing the viewer into the frame, of making the audience forget the boundaries of screen and tube to enter the scene.

The screen of TV is different from the screen of film. Film showings take place in a darkened room, with the viewer drawn into the frame. How different from the blending of TV into the total environment, literally a piece of furniture in the home. In both, however, audiences are made to ignore the screen's own inherent unrealities, which are as blatant as those of the stage.

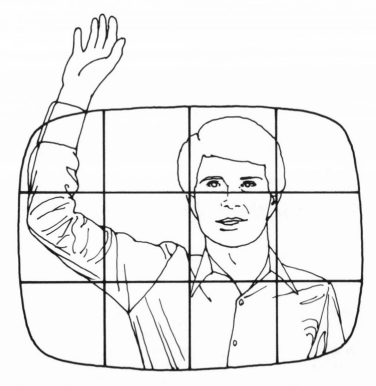

Illustration 1

SHAPE, SIZE AND RESOLUTION

In visual media, frame size is called *aspect ratio.* The aspect ratio of TV never varies: it is always three by four. That is, three units high and four units wide. Film maintained this aspect ratio through the forties, until wide screen formats became standard.

A common mistake in beginning media production is to confuse this frame with the rectangle of the stage. The result of this misunderstanding is action played frontally, as though on a stage. Such movement emphasizes the edges of the frame, rather than creating the impression of a real, three-dimensional scene. TV's three-by-four frame size limits directors' and actors' possibilities in many ways. An arm stretched up over the head will go out of the frame. To capture the gesture, the camera operator has to widen the shot, thereby losing the impact of facial expression. The solution for the performer might be to find another smaller gesture—for instance, pushing the shoulders back instead of stretching the arm. *(See illustration #1)*

Gestures, movement and grouping must be constructed within the ratio of this given frame. To show the entire body of a standing person next to a sitting person, one has to widen the shot. Taking a photograph of the same scene, one would be tempted to turn the camera sideways to reverse the aspect ratio. In TV one is stuck with the proportions of the screen image.

Relatively poor resolution is another problem TV presents for those who attempt to create the illusion of reality. TV's poor resolution means subtle, small details in wide or long shots are not encouraged. When a wide shot is used, audio cues direct the viewers' attention, or close-ups quickly dissect the wide shot and reveal the background. Other problems are the small screen, compared to that of film, and the competing realities in the viewing space that film excludes in the movie house.

Compared to film, TV is a mere information machine, devoid of sensual beauty. However, the manipulation of visual images through lighting and lens selection in both film and TV has the same foundations, although the effect may not be identical. Lighting and lens choices are critical in creating the illusion of three dimensions, in providing compositional balance and rhythm, in creating mood and in drawing attention to part of the frame. The actor has to understand the fundamentals of lighting and lenses because these choices have a practical effect on performance.

LIGHTING

To understand lighting, you have to begin to look at shadows. There are natural shadows on your face. For example, a light from above to your left will throw shadows under your nose on the right and under your chin, along your neck and shoulder. The closer this light is to pointing directly into your face, the less shadows it will cast. The further it is moved to the left, the more shadows it will cast. These shadows reveal your face in all its three-dimensional quality, including irregularities. The light that throws strong distinct shadows is called *hard light* and is similar to direct sunlight. It is distinguished from soft light, which is diffused or reflected, similar to the light on a hazy day. The aging starlet demands soft light to minimize the lines on her face.

The principle of three-point lighting for simple photographic portraits is the foundation for lighting in all visual media. The *key light* is a hard light from the front that is the primary source of illumination. Across from it, behind the head and about 30 degrees to the side, the *back light* gives solid form by outlining the body and making it stand out from the background. To create a contrast between the person and the background, the lighting on the background is usually at least 50 percent less bright than key and back lights. Finally, the *fill* is added from the front, opposite the key light. The fill is a soft light that fills in the deep shadows of the key without throwing any shadows of its own on the other side of the body. The purpose of the fill is not to eliminate totally the key light's shadows, which would flatten the image, but to soften them to the point where they are not distracting.

Lighting a news or talk show could be as simple as that three-point formula. When you add movement and constantly changing positions, however, the lighting plan becomes complex and demanding for the actor. In a scene as simple as a person entering a room and sitting on a sofa, the performer would have to know where the lights were focused, and how to sit in the exact position of focus, so that the key, back, and fill lights waiting for his or her face would not hit the shoulder instead.

In a complex scene, some lighting instruments will serve dual purposes. In a shot where you are facing a man, your back light could pass over your shoulder to become his key light. The danger is obvious: if you move out of your marked position, you'll block his principal source of illumination, leaving him only the fill light. Since the fill light is usually significantly less intense than the key light and doesn't show distinct shadows, he would appear strikingly different from you when the director cuts from close-up to close-up. *(See illustration # 2)*

Understanding these lighting principles for the performer and lighting director is like knowing the primary colors for the painter. The lighting director is an artist painting with light and shadows to create patterns and mood that help to interpret the narrative. The choices are governed by taste and not by science. Some of the choices can be worked out in advance, but every face and body is different, and the lighting has to be adjusted specifically for the individual. Keep this in mind as you sit for experiments with the lighting. These experiments don't mean the technical staff is incompetent. This sort of work is as critical as your own rehearsal to the quality of the final product.

Visual media do not capture reality, rather, they interpret it. For example, deep eye sockets lit with a key light placed high will appear dark and intense. By lowering the key light the sockets are flattened and appear less brooding. Lighting creates a mood just as much as an actor's voice or gesture, sometimes more so. There is lighting that tries to imitate real light sources: the sun through the window, the lamp by the bed, the bare bulb in the seedy hotel room and the flashing neon sign outside the window. Realism of this sort, with its silhouettes and deep shadows, can appear more artful on the screen than a more evenly balanced lighting that brings out details and uses shading to give a sense of solid depth.

The general lighting of an information show is intended simply to present clear images that don't confuse the viewer with multiple shadows. This lighting tends to be flat but usually has enough back light to create planes within the scene. What the lighting director is aiming for

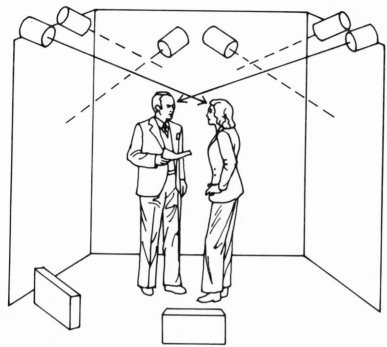

Illustration 2

is a natural effect on this kind of show. Without showing any real source of light in an obviously constructed setting, the lighting is designed *not* to be noticed by the viewer, but to be continuous, bright, filled out, to draw the viewers' eyes to the faces of the talent.

Sit-coms, soap operas, and most commercials are lit in the same way, solving the more complex problems of bringing out settings and properties while keeping the lighting balanced for actor movement. Some action and dramatic shows supplement or imitate real effects. Other variety—music and dance—shows work with abstract patterns and decorative lighting.

LENSES

Lenses are another part of the TV production that are used to manipulate reality. One lens will make a small room look large; another will flatten prominent cheekbones; another will make an actor running down a street seem to be jogging in place. Lenses collect light and focus it on the TV tube in the camera where light values are translated to electronic signals. The distance between the lens and the camera tube is called the *focal length.* For the performer, the crucial distinctions between lenses are those involving focal length.

Illustration 3

The most important difference in lenses is in the area of coverage. The longer the lens, the less of a scene is taken in. A *wide-angle* lens has a short focal length. An extreme wide angle, a *fish-eye* lens, can take up to 180 degrees. The distortions of the fish-eye clearly exaggerate characteristics of all wide-angle lenses. The wide-angle lens enlarges the foreground of a subject and creates depth. The wide angle is often used in TV to make a small set appear normal. But if you study soap opera, for example, you'll see how few steps it takes for someone to cross a room. Because the lens exaggerates the distance, actors moving at a normal rate will appear to be moving very quickly. Two steps will take them from a doorway into the center of what appears to be a spacious bedroom.

The long lens or *narrow-angle* lens has the opposite characteristics: it compresses space. In a wide-angle shot, a vase of flowers will loom far in front of an actor on a couch. In a narrow-angle view of the same scene, the vase will be flattened next to the talent *(see Illustration 3)*. Action seems slower because true distance is under-reported. A fast-moving car will seem to take an infinity as it approaches you.

Normal lenses, in between the wide angle and the narrow angle, come close to what our eyes would see from the same distance. But the audience can accept an unnatural perspective, and it is often necessary to use wider and narrower angles. The long lens is often needed in shooting outside to get close to a subject. And the short lens is often needed to take in a fuller scene without cutting several views of it together.

There are three primary reasons for using lenses of varying focal lengths. The first is to manipulate the scene, making it smaller or larger. The second and third reasons relate to space and time, especially in the studio production situation. You may not be able to get a camera close enough to a person because other equipment or settings are in the way. You may not be able to get a camera fast enough to grab the shot you want. Studio needs for different shots, gotten quickly and within strict space limitations, were one of the main reasons for the development of the *zoom*, or, as it is properly called, the *variable focal length* lens. All TV camera carry a zoom lens that allows a range from wide to normal to narrow focal lengths.

As you zoom in from a wide angle to a narrow angle, the area in which an actor can move and still remain in focus gets smaller. In one scene, the director might say, "We begin with a wide shot as you reach for the ringing phone, and then zoom into a close-up when you realize the Heavy Breather is on the other end." The narrow-angle close-up at the end of the zoom demands that you stay precisely in place: a six-inch leaning movement could put your face out of focus. On a wide shot, however, you might lean back, stretch out your arm, or take a step in the wrong direction and still stay in focus. This measurement of the area in focus is called *depth of field.* Performers should know the depth of field at their disposal in each shot or scene.

The performer's inventiveness has to be exercised within these technical boundaries and within the director's shot choices. An interesting shuffle of the feet is not worth much in a waist shot. Neither is a glint in the eye when the face goes unlit because you turned your head out of the key. The more that actors and performers understand the technical choices being made—and their implications—the more creative they can be.

Imagine a wide-angle shot with a woman's face in the foreground looking into the camera. In the background is the full body of her mother. The wide angle enlarges the daughter's face and catches the slightest furrowing of her brow, a gesture that would be lost if used by the mother. The mother needs to use a larger gesture to show her concern: she leans forward, turns her head, opens her mouth, pulls her shoulders up. When she takes the step forward to touch her daughter's arm, she takes slow, small steps to fit the spatial perspective.

Working within the frame and bowing to the demands of the lighting designer, director and camera operator may at first seem to place constraints on the actor's creativity and reason for being: acting. Yet if the actor wants to create the same illusion of reality he or she does on stage, and to draw in the audience, the actor must perform within the limitations of the medium. Knowing the blocking, lighting and the lens requirements ultimately gives the actor more freedom and more choice.

SOUND RECORDING

The performer also needs to understand the problems of sound recording and the basic differences between microphones. In some cases you will be asked to control your voice within the equipment limits. And, just as you have to hit the toe marks for camera shots, you also have to be blocked for audio pick-up. TV or film audio effects can emphasize the natural voice, the real whisper, the croak and the mumble in a way that is unthinkable on the proscenium stage, where the last row has to catch each syllable. But each vocal effect has to be planned and the sound manipulated.

The initial problem for stage actors is controlling their dynamic range within the limits tolerated by the recording equipment. This means that wide variations in volume—soft or quiet or loud—are difficult to record. Our ears respond with much more sensitivity to dynamic range than do tape recorders.

It is helpful to understand how volume is measured. First, volume is relative. It is controlled by microphone placement and amplification as well as by how the actor speaks. Volume is measured in decibels, or "db's," which have a logorhythmic progression. This means that every three decibels the sound doubles or halves. The sound recordist uses this scale of decibels as a relative measure of volume change. Starting at 0 db, plus-3 db is twice the amplification, minus-3 db is half the amplification, minus-6 is one-fourth, minus-9 is one-eighth, and so on.

On the audio mix panel, where several audio (microphone and other source) inputs are monitored, and on the recording deck, there is a volume unit (VU) meter that reads both decibel change and percent of tape saturation. You'll notice in the illustration that 100 percent tape saturation and 0 db are the same. To the left of 0 db and 100 percent, the meter is in the black; to the right, it is in the red and registers an overload or distortion.

The dynamic range of sound recording is very limited compared to that of our own ears. The sound recordist can boost for a soft, quiet sound, but then a loud sound will overload the system and become distorted. If the sound recordist drops the amplification to handle the loud sounds, then the soft ones will disappear.

Technicians refer to signal-to-noise ratio, S/N. The fuller the tape saturation, the cleaner the signal. Your voice is being recorded as a signal over noise that is inherent in the system. The fuller the tape saturation, the higher the signal-to-noise ratio, and the less noise heard.

Sound recordists try to keep the VU meter (see illustration 4) just into the red, as close to 100 percent as possible. Normal talking range is around −8 db, around 60 percent, allowing for a dynamic range as your voice gets louder or softer, peaking at the red. The sound recordist tries to follow your level, getting as full a saturation as possible without distortion. This is called *riding gain.* The recordist can easily ride gain for abrupt changes in sound levels if they are expected and written into the script, with a clear cue to drop down for the shriek of horror that rises out of the whispers. On the other hand, sudden low volume can be gradually boosted back to a normal level. The sudden changes from loud to soft will make an impact, but the signal degradation inherent in low levels will be avoided as the recordist raises the level back up to peak at 100 percent.

In post-production, during editing and transmission, TV sound is enormously limited and compressed. The compressor is a device that boosts all the low sounds up to a very narrow dynamic range. The limiter is a device that cuts loud sounds off before they can distort. Limiters and compressors can be used in the original recording as an automatic gain control, but this eliminates the selective control of the sound recordist.

A useful exercise for you, the beginning TV actor, is to deliver lines while listening to yourself with headsets and watching the VU meter. This exercise will give you an immediate understanding of your dependence on volume for expressing emotion and a gauge for the limits that will make your voice work in recording. You'll be surprised at the volume change possible within one word; an attack on the first syllable will drop off in the second, presenting a difficult recording problem. In most cases the sound recordist should be totally responsible for riding gain to record your voice, no matter what demands you make on his or her skill. However, there are limits. The most important factor to the recordist is that your audio level be relatively predictable, from rehearsal or script. The recordist will take a sample level from you to get an idea of how to ride gain on your voice. The level you give has to be exactly as you intend to deliver the lines during takes. This will be easiest if you use your actual lines when reading for sound levels.

The one common case where a recordist will ask you to raise or lower your volume is when two or more talents are using the same microphone. When recording with one mike, there is no way to compensate for voices with large differences in volume as they carry on a conversation. As the recordist takes your audio level, he or she will also make choices in mike selection and placement, and will consider the need to alter your pitch. If you understand these choices, you'll be able to make your voice more effective in the medium.

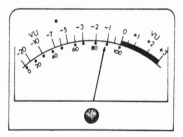

Illustration 4

Illustration 5

MICROPHONES

Sensitivity to volume is determined by the microphone's sound-generating element. The majority of microphones used in TV rely on two kinds of sound-generating elements. One kind is the dynamic or movable coil mike, the other is the condenser mike. The dynamic mike is less sensitive to sound waves than the condenser. It takes more force to move the element, which is a diaphragm attached to a coil that is attached to a magnet. In contrast, the condenser mike is extremely sensitive, with a mylar diaphragm much thinner and easier to move than the coil-magnet element in the dynamic mike. The condenser has two plates charged by a power source, usually batteries. The pressure of your voice in sound waves varies the distance between the plates. This variation creates the electronic signal recorded on the tape.

The condenser microphone is widely used in most video situations because of its greater sensitivity to volume. The Sony ECM-50 is a tiny condenser mike that you will recognize on the lapels of most newscasters. There are many brands of microphones, both dynamic and condenser, with slight differences in design that affect their sensitivity and fidelity. The sound-generating element can be separated from the power supply of the condenser mike, and therefore the condenser mikes can be much smaller and less obtrusive than dynamic mikes *(in illustration 5)*.

The condenser mike is more fragile than the dynamic mike. Precisely because it is more sensitive, it does not lend itself to hand-held use. Both dynamic and condenser mikes have especially designed models for hand-holding, both encased in a shock-mount that insulates them from the rubbing of your hand. The dynamic mike is more easily designed for hand-holding, and therefore is often used by the location reporter in front of a government building or at the scene of a crime, when interviewing a witness or summarizing an event—or on any other

occasion. Although some condenser mikes are built with a shield-casing that allows for hand-holding, they are for the most part susceptible to rough handling and loud sounds. For that reason, singers commonly use the dynamic mike, since gesturing, shaking and blasting into the mike from a distance of only an inch or two would be disastrous to any condenser mike.

Both condenser and dynamic mikes are designed in models that can be attached to clothes—to a tie or a lapel or a shirt front—or hand-held, used on a stand, suspended on a pole, hung or hidden. Small mikes, called lavaliers, can be hidden in clothes with the cord taped under the clothing. If hidden, they usually have to be cushioned by tape, moleskin, or foam; condenser mikes in particular pick up the rubbing of even the softest cloth, and make polyester sound like thunder. Lavalier mikes have taken the place of most desk-stand mikes because there is less chance of picking up table noise, tapping and such, or the shuffle of papers. Lavaliers are sensitive to touch, and the recordist will warn you not to pound your chest if a mike is attached to it, or to stroke or tug on the mike cable or cord, since that, too, carries a noise.

Both condenser and dynamic mikes can be suspended from above and turned and tilted to follow a scene. This technique enables the recordist to get good sound from each speaker with the microphone out of the camera frame. Since the mike has to be tilted up for wide shots, which puts it far away—six feet or even more from the mouth— condenser mikes are most often used in this capacity. However, even the most sensitive mikes can only be pushed so far; an actor who misses a mark and is ten instead of five feet away from where the boom operator expects him to be may ruin a take. The equipment operator is responsible for following the action, and some directors do block actors very loosely. In the best of production worlds, the interest in good sound, and the responsibility for getting it, would be shared.

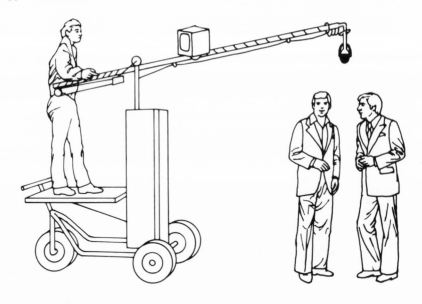

Illustration 6   Large Platform Boom

Studio sound equipment comes in a variety of shapes and arrangements. There is a large platform boom, and the fishpole, which is a medium-sized boom that offers a lot of flexibility, including the possibility of booming from below and walking with the actor to follow the action *(see illustration 6)*. The platform boom is used in large-studio dramatic situations to cover sets from above. *All in the Family,* for example, uses two large platform booms, a fishpole to catch dialogue the platforms can't reach and hidden or hanging mikes for lines delivered from a carefully blocked position inaccessible to the boom or fishpole operators. Booms and fishpoles have a cueing head that allows the operator to not only tilt and retract the mike but also to rotate it, usually on a 320 degree axis. This means that a conversation can be covered by cueing the mike toward one speaker or another without the operator or the boom-arm moving.

There is also the wireless mike, which is most often used for location shooting where a fishpole or cord could not be kept out of the picture. The wireless mike is usually a small condenser lavalier, like the Sony ECM-50, attached by a cord to a transmitter about the size of a pack of cigarettes and weighing four or five ounces. The transmitter usually broadcasts a signal on a TV channel that is not being used in the area, and the signal is picked up by a receiver that can be as much as a thousand feet away. The transmitter can be put in a pocket, taped to a leg, secured to the small of the back with an ace bandage or sewn into the clothes. It's always important that the cable be carefully anchored, since

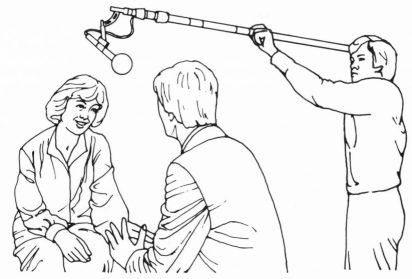

Fishpole

rustling clothes noise is always a problem. Wireless mikes are improving all the time, but even the newest are susceptible to interference from other transmitters. Radio signals, airplanes, taxis and such can ruin a take or make the use of a wireless mike impossible. Some hand-held wireless mikes have the transmitter built in, but they are used for stage performers and night club acts and aren't suitable for recording.

Both condenser and dynamic microphones are designed with a variety of pickup patterns. A two-dimensional map, called a polar response graph, shows the area of coverage *(see illustration 7)*. The omni-directional mike covers 360 degrees. This full pattern of coverage is commonly used on the lavalier or lapel mikes, on some hand-held interviewing mikes and on video portapaks. Since this pattern gets everything, it is useful in certain kinds of taping situations. On the

Illustration 7

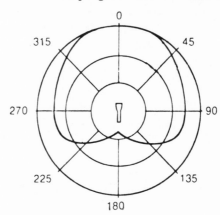

portapak, its use means that one person can shoot and be sure of getting audio coverage. The hand-held dynamic-omni, which is not as sensitive to breath pops, can be held very close to your mouth to exclude surrounding noise. In contrast, the omni-condenser lavalier is set up to be very sensitive, like a hair-trigger. It has to be placed near the collar-bone, away from the resonance of the chest, usually about six inches below the chin. But, every *body* is different; a good sound recordist will experiment with exact placement. The performer should speak across, and not directly into, the head of the omni-directional mike. The performer does not need to, and should not, look down at the mike.

The omni, however, is not always the most desirable pickup pattern. If the mike is suspended from a boom to keep it out of the shot, there is no reason for it to pick up sound out of the set or away from the action. In fact, it is preferable to reject the inevitable background noise created by the crowd of people and equipment.

The cardioid pattern mike was developed to reject noise from the rear. The cardioid mike has a heart-shaped pattern wide enough to pick up a conversation back and forth between two people. The cardioid is used more often than is the narrower, uni-directional mike, which has even greater rejection from the rear and both sides. In fact, the uni-directional has to be carefully aimed at the performer's mouth. Often called a shotgun because of its long barrel, this mike is frequently used on outside location work because a voice can be picked out from a crowd of surrounding noises, such as traffic. Cardiod and uni-directional mikes must be held or placed six inches to a foot away from the mouth, otherwise the voice will distort. This distortion, called the proximity effect, drops out the mid-range of the voice and emphasizes high-pitched and very low-pitched sounds. This is one reason why most of the dynamic mikes used by singers are also omni-directional.

Another pickup pattern less frequently used is the bi-directional, or figure-eight. This mike pattern works well for a face-on conversation with noise rejection to both sides. However, this mike can only be used if the actors are stationary: it can't be angled, and would most likely be used when the mike is shown in the shot or hidden between the performers. The varieties of pickup patterns are infinite, and within each of the broad categories—omni, cardioid, shotgun, and bi-, there are other differences according to manufacturer and model. It is up to the sound recordist to specify the requirements of the mike you are using.

Every mike responds differently to pitch. The number of times a sound wave occurs per second is called its frequency, measured in cycles, or hertz (abbreviated Hz). The more bass a voice is, the less Hz. The more treble a voice is, the more Hz. Our ears hear approximately from 20 to 16,000 Hz. The human voice is concentrated around 200 to 5,000

Hz. Our best hearing is around 3,500 Hz and falls off at higher and lower frequencies. The quieter the sound, the faster our hearing falls off in both directions.

Every mike comes with a frequency response graph that documents its ability to record at each point on the frequency. In most cases, a sound recordist looks for a mike that will give a flat response, that is, pick up with equal sensitivity at each frequency level. The dynamic mike is less sensitive at high-pitch ranges because of its heavy sound-generating element. The low, bass end of the voice moves a lot of air, while the high end, the piccolo, moves hardly any. In some instances, it becomes necessary to cut off or augment a portion of the available frequency. In a scene shot in a boomy room with high concrete ceilings and walls, you would want to cut off the lower-end frequencies. This is done by choosing a mike designed to cut off frequencies below 100 or 150 Hz. The sound recordist can also use filters added to the mike that do the same job. The filters can then be removed after the particular need is filled. The opposite effect can be achieved by attaching an attenuator to the mike. The attenuator will emphasize an area of the frequency.

For performers, this means their own pitch can be manipulated, dropping out the squeaky high sounds of one voice, the bassiness of another. The equalizer, a panel of filters and attenuators, allows the recordist to manipulate several selected areas of the frequency at the same time for one signal. Working outside, the recordist might use an equalizer to drop down the auto traffic noise rumble, boost the voice, and boost the birds singing in the background. In re-recording a conversation between several people in a rapid exchange, it is possible to use an equalizer to bring up each person's pitch when talking, or, if several were talking, the recordist could emphasize one character over another.

A more mechanical way of altering the microphone's recording is to place filters made of foam or plastic screen directly on the microphone. A small foam filter, called a pop filter, will catch the plosive sounds of "p" and "b," which can create a rush of air that will blast against the sound-generating element. The sound recordist usually has a bag filled with a large collection of different qualities and densities of foams. Some are designed for high winds outside, but even in the studio a wind-screen will be used on the boom mike to diffuse the rush of wind caused by the movement of the boom arm.

SUMMARY OF AUDIO DO'S AND DON'TS

Let the sound recordist, mixer, boom operator do their jobs.
Be aware of how you are being miked. With the hand-held

or lavalier mike, know your movement limits, how much cable you have. Be conscious of mike placement: don't tug at your coat if the mike is tacked to its lapel; don't finger the mike cable.

With hand-held mikes, remember that condenser mikes will distort if held too close to the mouth, but that you should speak into them. Omni's can be, and often should be, held close to the mouth to exclude extraneous sounds. If you're interviewing someone with a hand-held mike, remember to point the mike toward him or her when he or she is talking and toward yourself when you're talking.

Remember that all mikes require careful handling, all are in some degree fragile instruments; be careful where and how you put them down.

With a boom or fishpole mike, don't put the back of your head between the mike and your mouth; don't speak downstage if the boom operator is prepared to mike you upstage.

Give the sound recordist a predictable reading, tested in rehearsals or level checks. Remember that in some cases you will have to be ready to drop or raise your volume to match your voice with another performer when you are both being covered by the same boom mike.

3

FILLING THE SCREEN:
Composition and Shot Choice

Since the first film images were recorded in 1895, the screen or projection surface has had its own scale and power. The screen uncovers things too large for our attention—train-station crowds, parading armies—as well as things too small for our attention—the unmailed letter crumpled and dropped to the floor, the precise action of peeling an orange. The technical limitations of television, however, have encouraged a specialized set of visual conventions. As we noted in Chapter 1, these conventions evolved because of television's relatively small screen and lower quality visual resolution—the 4 by 3 aspect ratio of the TV picture—as well as TV's function as an information or "talking" source.

Such factors have encouraged the development of TV production styles that have roots in the dialogue-based film styles of the 1940s. Knowing the visual and stylistic conventions of television, as well as the related working vocabulary, is vital to the TV performer's work. The dominant images of television revolve around speaking performers and are usually described in relation to the performer's body. The majority of shots consist of close-ups, couples and small groupings. One common series of shot descriptions based on natural body points includes: the full shot, the face shot, the shoulder shot, the bust shot, the waist shot and the knee shot. Another series may include the extreme close-up (ECU), the close-up (CU), and the medium close-up (MCU). Couple groupings are usually referred to as the two-shot (2S) and small groups as the three-shot or four-shot (3S, 4S). *(See illustration 8.)*

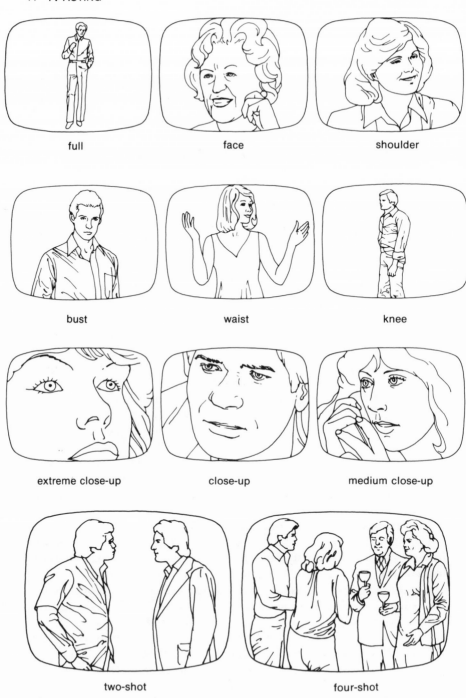

full

face

shoulder

bust

waist

knee

extreme close-up

close-up

medium close-up

two-shot

four-shot

Illustration 8

Illustration 9

The exact TV shot categories are not standardized; in fact, one director's close-up will be another's extreme close-up. The position of the performers' bodies also changes the effect of the shot tremendously. A two-shot using both profiles is quite different from one using two three-quarter faces or a profile and a full face *(see illustration 9)*. In the over-the-shoulder two-shot, the shoulder, arm or back of the head of one performer frames the open face of another, creating still another effect *(see illustration 10)*. The wide shot, with its great depth of field, can be used to present several planes of action—for example, to cover a whole room and include background activity in the hallway. This layering of activity, with several planes of characters in depth, poses

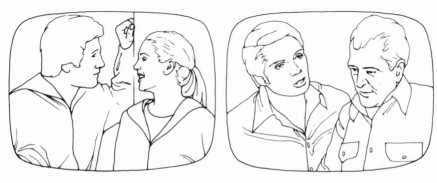

Illustration 10

difficult problems for the actor. As noted in Chapter 2, if the actor is in the background, movements must become broader than those in the foreground. Knowing where you stand, literally, in the frame, and in the depth of field, dictates how you will move and act.

Changes in shots and focal length may seem arbitrary until you realize how camera placement—shot size, angle and movement— interprets a scene. As a performer, you have to ask what the camera will be seeing and what you want it to see. What image is necessary to carry the information you, the actor, wish to convey?

Visual change on the TV screen takes place in three ways: the actor moves, the frame moves or the frame is switched or edited. Actor movement will be discussed in Chapter 5, editing in Chapter 6. Frame, or camera movement, can involve moving just the camera or the *pedestal* (a tripod with wheels on which the camera sits), or both. Moving only the camera laterally is called *panning,* as in "pan left" or "pan right to follow her as she crosses the room." Pointing the camera up or down is called *tilting,* as in "tilt up a little, you're cutting off her forehead too much."

Changing the height of the camera is termed *pedestaling* up or down. Pedestaling down and tilting up, a low-angle shot, can make a man with a high forehead look bald. By looking down, however, the performer shows his hair and changes his image. The below-eye-level shot of a news commentator allows him to fill the frame and look down authoritatively at the viewers. On the other hand, a low-angle shot also accentuates the neck, shows a double chin and, for most performers, usually won't be as flattering as a shot pedestaled slightly above eye level and tilted down *(see illustration 11).* All these camera positions and movements can be used while the pedestal itself is being pushed and pulled—in, back or to either side or arched in a semicircle. The pedestal movements require another set of terms.

Usually the camera operator *dollies* in or out, as in "dolly out from a two-shot to a wide shot as they leave the room." Moving the pedestal laterally is called *trucking* or *crabbing. Tracking* describes all pedestal movement. It is a term taken from film production, where tracks are actually laid for the camera pedestal to roll on. For maximum freedom, however, the camera can be mounted on a crane with a boom arm that suspends the camera so that it can smoothly change both height and position, sweeping down and in or up and out. Moving the camera's position around and past objects or people creates a sense of three-dimensional depth on the flat screen. Crane shots are often used to open dramas. By craning from a high angle—a bird's-eye-view—into a scene, the viewer is drawn into the frame and passes across the rectangular line of the stage.

While the camera is moving and changing the context of the frame, actors have to consider what parts of their bodies are actually in the frame. Think of the common scene where "she" enters "his" room. *(See*

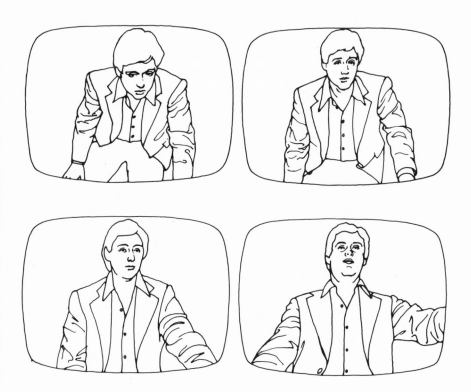

Illustration 11

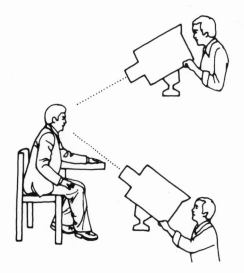

Illustration 12

illustration 12.) Shot one would be a *close-up*, a face shot of him, the camera *pedestaled* up and *tilted* down. His head looks up in response to the sound of the door opening. Shot two is a *waist shot:* half of her body is seen closing the door and moving across the room in front of a background of furniture. The camera *pans* beside this half-body, leading her so that the distance from her nose to the edge of the frame stays the same. She arrives at his head, which now has shoulders, and her hand reaches toward him in the *two-shot* that has now been created. The camera zooms in slightly to tighten the *two-shot* as her hand approaches his cheek. Shot three is a *medium close-up, shoulder shot.* We see his head alone again with a hand touching his cheek.

In this example, the actor's body is obviously fragmented. The actor must use the timing of the shots as well as the body parts in the frame to express the scene. Performers ideally should be as familiar as the director with the cutting or switching plan, or shooting script, as it is called. Whether you have your head to work with, or your shoulders, arm and head, or the back of your head is obviously critical to how you play a scene. You might begin a line of dialogue on a close-up and end it in a long shot. Working within the given shots, there is a wide range of actor/performer movement that will fill the frame. First you have to know what the shots are and how they will make you look. Vocabulary, especially describing body shots, presents an area of confusion for the actor and may require the director's clarification.

For non-dramatic shows, unpredictable talk-game shows and such, there is usually a format that specifies a set of shots within which you can work. On a *Meet the Press* program, for example, the guest was covered in a tight *shoulder shot* and a *waist shot*. He was seen at the opening and closing of the show in a *wide shot*—which included the *Meet the Press* logo and the three panelists plus moderator—as the announcer read the opening lines voice-over. After a *medium shot* of the moderator welcoming the viewers to the show, there was a switch to a *face shot* of the guest while the moderator narrated his background. The guest, thinking as a performer, could have "acted" for these two opening shots: in the wide shot, by looking up at the panelist closest to the camera, and, in the face shot, by keeping his head still, not bobbing, and using subdued facial reactions to the moderator's lines.

For the rest of the show, the camera for the guest was positioned on a platform opposite him and behind the panelist's background scenery flat, thus at a high angle. The guest used a lot of arm movement, but there was no way for him to know when he was in a *face shot,* when his arm movement was being expended without effect. It was up to the director to command the camera operator to get a shot that would include the guest's movement when it was expressive.

The high angle of the camera made the guest look small, and revealed the surface of his desk. He persisted in working against himself by making gestures at waist level near the desk top. The shot made the gestures obscure and furtive, and made him seem nervous. He was working at the bottom of the frame, drawing attention away from his face and down, emphasizing the high angle's effect of making him look small. At the same time, his gestures were hidden behind the stand-microphone on the desk. Had the guest/performer been aware of the angle of the shots, he could have changed his performance accordingly. Simpler gestures, below or to the side of his face, would have punctuated his arguments. Sweeping gestures, leaning back and looking up as he thought about the answers to a question or waiting out an interviewer's probe, could have combated the shrinking effect of the high angle.

Some directors will tell you how you fill the screen, some you have to ask, some won't answer, some don't know. Learning the camera operator's vocabulary is the first step in learning to relate to the camera and developing gestures to the size and scale of the image. These problems are the subject of the following chapters.

4

THE TV AUDIENCE:
Relating to the Camera and the Viewer

In many homes, the TV is turned on in the morning and turned off at bedtime. TV fills silence, entertains and provides the basic information about the world for most American families. Thirty million people watch a talk show like *The Merv Griffin Show,* fifteen million watch a midday soap opera and even an "unsuccessful" show such as a public affairs documentary may have a viewing audience of ten million people. The industry focuses on the number of viewers who watch each show because, after all, commercial broadcast TV is designed to guarantee the largest possible audience for each commercial message. Likewise, industrial training tapes and public information tapes are made because they are an economical way to reach a large audience through repeated showings.

This emphasis on audience size is often misleading to the performer. Thirty million viewers or ten thousand employees are not a reality to the performer. Most TV shows are viewed by one to five people sitting in their own home watching a small twelve- to twenty-inch screen in a box that is a piece of furniture. The TV is a familiar object in the living room, the kitchen, the bedroom, the conference room and the lecture hall. It does not command special attention. We do not go out to see TV; no lights are lowered or curtain raised to draw our attention to the beginning of a show. In fact, there is often something comic about gathering to watch a TV show in a formal setting. At most, we may go to a local bar or restaurant to watch a special news or sporting event on a large screen while we have dinner or a drink.

Illustration 13

Stage

Even training tapes or information tapes are often watched by only one person or a small group of people at any given time. Usually they are watched in a familiar setting. Many companies now have actually designed viewing rooms to be more "homelike" and less "theatrelike," while most libraries have individual viewing spaces. The mass TV audience does not really exist for the performers except as statistics.

A second reality that the performer must never forget, which was mentioned in Chapter 1, is that the TV audience member, unlike the film or theatre audience member, is often interrupted or engaged in another activity while watching. Conversations occur during shows, phone calls are answered and food breaks are taken. People sew, read, eat, draw, write, and do homework while watching TV. They may take notes during a training tape or ask questions. The performer is probably lucky to get 80 to 85 percent of his audience's attention. Therefore, when performers begin to work on TV, they should visualize clearly the real viewing audience for the show or tape being made. Even in a situation where there is a studio audience, the performer should never forget the home viewer, the one to five people gathered in a small room with the lights on, who may well be interrupted during the viewing or simultaneously engaged in another activity. Such an awareness will help the actor keep his or her performance in proper scale and serve as the basis for real communication with the audience.

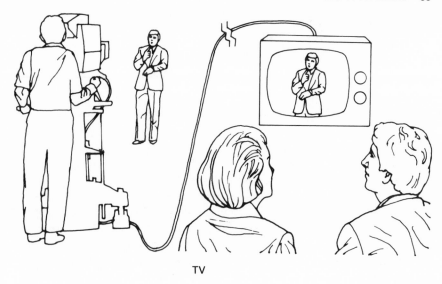

TV

How a performer reaches this viewing audience is a question of how he or she relates to the lens of the camera. The camera is the only eye the viewer has. In a stage or platform situation, the viewer can, within the limits of his seat, choose what he or she wishes to watch. In TV, the selection is made by whoever chooses the camera shots. The following diagram *(illustration 13)* may be helpful.

In the average TV studio, there are, of course, at least two cameras and often as many as five. The principle, however, remains the same: the eye of the viewer sees only the camera shot used in the final edit. What the performer shows the lens is all that is available to the viewer. As we explained in Chapter 1, shows are taped in many different ways. Some are recorded on four cameras and edited together. Others are recorded primarily on one camera while another camera records reaction shots and secondary shots. Some are shot line by line while others, shot with live audiences, are run in longer segments. In many cases, the performer is blocked for a specific camera and knows exactly which camera to play to. At other times, the director chooses not to furnish this information and simply chooses to record enough material to edit later. (See Chapter 9 for a discussion of work styles.) Whatever the situation, a successful TV performer is always aware of the position of the cameras, of the reality of the camera lens and of himself or herself as a performer who works inside a small frame. It is desirable to have the skill to play to a specific camera and to relate to the lens in a variety of ways.

There are three basic ways that a performer can relate to the lens. First, he or she can speak directly into the lens, and thus appear to be talking on a one-to-one basis with the viewer. This style of camera work is called "presentational." News shows, talk shows and public information tapes often use this technique. This technique may also be used in such a way as to make the camera lens appear to be the eyes of another character or interviewer. Second, the camera can be one member of the audience. In this technique, also used in talk shows and interview situations, the performer will look directly into the lens, but will not stop or allow the eyes to linger in the lens. These two techniques are often combined by talk show personalities—Johnny Carson for example—who wish to acknowledge the home viewing audience, the guest and the studio audience. Third, the performer may avoid making eye contact with the camera altogether. In other words, the frame is preserved between the viewer and the performer. The viewer is allowed to watch unacknowledged by the performer. Generally this is the technique used in all dramatic shows, in soap operas and in most situation comedies. It is, of course, the way in which an actor in a realistic stage play relates to the audience.

Each of these techniques presents specific problems for the performer. Many people find it extremely difficult to actually maintain eye contact with the camera lens. They watch the camera operator or the studio personnel and, even though they are staring toward the lens, do not really make eye contact with it in such a way as to contact the viewer. With the second technique, lingering a moment too long or stopping on the lens can give the effect of "mugging" for viewers. In the third case, even a moment of direct eye contact will seem amateurish and destroy the illusion. The third technique also presents the problem of "staying open" to the camera, allowing it to watch, to come into the performance. Just as a stage actor opens to the audience, so must the TV actor. Even in interview shows, where guests are expected to talk only to the host, the effect is more pleasing if the bodies of the guests and host do not close out the camera. If the bodies and faces are consistently turned away from the camera, then the viewer feels like an intruder and unimportant.

One of the most helpful concepts for relating to the viewer, whatever technique is being used, is to think of a triangle (see illustration 14) composed of, at one apex, the camera lens (i.e., the viewer); at another, the performer; and at the third, the other characters, the studio audience, the host, the product being sold or the script being read. As long as the performer is aware of this triangle, the viewer will not be excluded, the product forgotten nor the guest ignored. In some way, whether by eye contact, line of gaze or body position, the performer should attempt to relate to the other two points at all times.

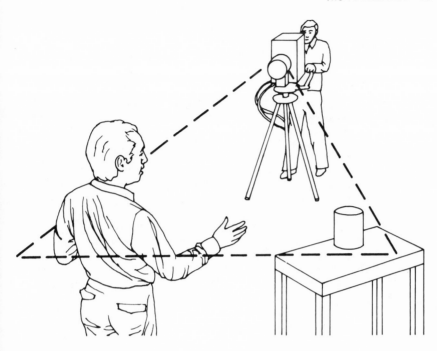

Illustration 14

EXERCISES

The exercises listed below are designed to provide specific help with problems of relating to the camera:

Exercise I: Specific TV observations are most helpful. Watch TV without the sound turned on: imagine the placement of each camera. Watch a news show, a soap opera, a situation comedy and a talk show. Visualize yourself in front of the cameras on each type of show, and imagine how you would relate to the camera for each shot.

Exercise II: This exercise requires a camera, a monitor and an R.F. adaptor or cable to connect the monitor and the video tape recording deck. The monitor should be placed where another person can watch, but where you cannot see the screen. You should speak directly into the camera while the viewer gives you feedback about the quality of your eye contact with the lens. With this technique, you can adjust your camera relationship until you succeed in discovering what it feels like to make direct contact with the lens rather than merely looking toward it.

This exercise also develops the ability to discipline your eyes to maintain a specific focus. On camera, even a momentary accidental flicker of the eyes toward a crew member, for example, is visible. Breaks in eye contact are necessary, but they must be natural, as in conversation. If no camera is available, you can gain some skill by creating a disc the size of a lens, placing it on a wall, and trying to maintain contact with it as if there were a viewer on the other side. Break contact purposely to think or to punctuate an idea.

Exercise III: You need the ability to direct your performance from one camera to another. Practice this skill by placing three chairs in different places in a room as if they were cameras; give each a number.

Step #1. Decide on a story to tell or a monologue to deliver, and block your presentation to be directed at a specific camera at a specific moment. Practice until you can easily change cameras at the designated moments without losing your concentration on the material.

Step #2. Using a story or monologue, have a friend serve as the floor director and indicate to which "camera" (chair) you should direct your performance. Your story or monologue should be at least three minutes long so that you can logically change "cameras" several times. In actuality, studio cutting is done on movement (see Chapter 6). You should, therefore, discover logical movements to help you change from one "camera" to another. Practice until the signals to change no longer disrupt your concentration on the material or the camera.

Exercise IV: To practice the triangle concept, select a product to demonstrate or sell and select a point in the room as the camera, or set up a chair. Work until you can perform the demonstration or deliver the "sales pitch" without losing sight of either the camera lens or the product for more than one or two seconds. Insofar as possible, keep both in your line of vision.

Exercise V: Tell a story to a friend who is sitting to your right. Place the camera or a stand-in for it to your left. Do not look at the camera; look at the other person. However, never close your body to the camera or forget the lens. Insofar as possible, let the camera stay in your peripheral vision.

SUMMARY

TV shows are not designed primarily for a live audience. If a live audience is present, it is generally there (except in such non-studio situations as sporting events, parades or public news conferences) to improve the quality of the show for the TV viewer. Even where live events are being recorded, the TV director's focus is on the home viewer or the consumer who will use the tape at a later time. Thus a TV performer works primarily for the lens of the camera. The more a TV performer relates to the camera, ceases to see the camera either as an intruder or a "Xerox" machine and allows it to be the primary audience member, the better the performance will be.

5

WORKING ON THE SCREEN:
Scale and Gesture

The scale or "size" of a performance necessary for effective stage work is generally a liability on the screen. The actor must reduce normal theatre gestures and control stage projection. The unpracticed and untrained performer, who would be disastrous on the professional stage, may well have an initial advantage over stage professionals in screen work. Theatre training and experience encourages a type of performance that appears overdone and unnatural under the close scrutiny of the camera.

Stage actors have learned, and can learn, an immense amount from film and TV documentaries. Studying audio and visual recordings of "real people" going about their daily activities and talking about themselves is extremely helpful in creating fuller characterizations, especially in finding the details of daily life that are critical on the screen and go unseen on the stage. The untrained "real person" can often present a natural image on the screen that few actors can approach. As the advertising business has demonstrated, there can be something startlingly honest about a "real person's" testimony on a thirty-second soap commercial; in screen terms, such performance can be on a par with or even excel that of a great actor.

In fact, amateurs have played important roles in some of the great fiction films. While the amateur doesn't have to shed a learned stage technique, the screen doesn't simply and faithfully record real life. The editor of documentaries, and the director who coaches non-actors, are in fact limited by working with people unskilled in screen acting techniques. It is easier to work with screen actors than with "real people," and it is possible to get more complicated work from them. The screen actor is able to generally scale down from a stagey performance, creating gestures that fit the size of the shot within an illogical working space that seldom reflects the action as it would occur in "real life."

In Chapter 3, we described the actor's relationship to fragmentation—now a head, now a hand, only occasionally a full body. To go several steps further, actors have to understand 1) size as it relates to properties and movement, 2) the constantly changing space they have to work in and 3) how gestures are created within the frame of each shot as size and space change.

SIZE IN THE TV IMAGE

On the screen, size is relative. A grand piano that fills the screen in one shot can be followed in the next shot by a foot that would seem just as large as the piano without visual references such as the piano pedals to indicate its relative size in the scene. The relativity of size is the basis for visual jokes that come out of an understanding of the medium. In the next shot, for instance, it might be revealed that the foot is, in fact, a giant's foot or that the piano is a child's toy. Viewers expect these changes in size and perspective—now studying, now glimpsing people and objects from all sides. Contemporary screen work has become progressively more sophisticated in the complexity of images viewers must follow.

Size is also relative within a single shot and depends upon camera placement. Imagine this scene, which you've watched in a hundred variations: In the foreground, an immense phone is ringing. It fills the entire left third of the frame. A body is on the floor in the middle of the frame and, in the background, the detective stands in the doorway. The detective's head is actually quite smaller than the phone, which dominates the frame. But if this scene were shot from the reverse angle, from the doorway, the telephone becomes an insignificant object, a piece of decor. It doesn't visually ask the narrative questions: "Who's calling?" "Why?" *(see illustration 15.)*

It is important to remember that the foreground is always enlarged to some degree, even when shooting with a "normal" lens angle. The actor has to adjust for this scale. The background gesture of the cop in the doorway, as he recoils at seeing the body, is broader than the flicker of disdain that we see in a medium close-up after he's crossed the room and answered the phone. The actor is now sharing the foreground with the phone, and the smallest gesture stands out. Even how he holds the phone is crucial—gripped, cradled, twisted away from his mouth. When the person on the other end hangs up, does the actor suspend the phone

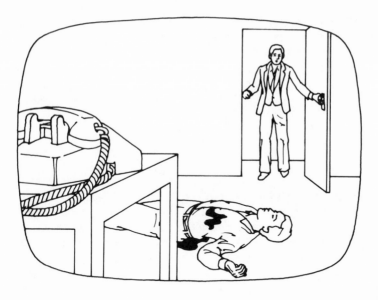

Illustration 15

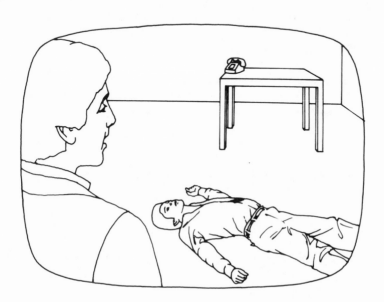

for a second, rested against his chest or held toward the camera, before he slams it down? The space he has to work in is very tight. His leg has to touch the table the phone is on. His elbow has to stay flat against his side or it will obscure the corpse in the background. At the beginning of the shot by the doorway, the actor's eye-line wasn't significant; at the end; on the phone, the viewer catches every batted eyelash and reads it for significance.

RELATIVE POSITIONS

The space actors have to work in as they create frames is constantly changing. Stage actors will be upset by how close they have to play some scenes. The flat TV image emphasizes the smallest distance between characters. On a panel show such as *Meet the Press,* the panelists are sitting with not more than an inch between their chairs. Toe-to-toe, nose-to-nose contact can look "normal" on the screen; the psychological distance that you think is demanded by a storyline can put you "abnormally" far apart.

The actor also has to learn to create space with posture and with body position rather than with floor distance. Body language becomes crucial. The head back, the back arched, the arm over the back of the couch—all give the illusion of distance.

Camera movement can, by itself, define space for the actors as well. For example, the camera can arc-dolly around actors in a two-shot, creating space between them and emphasizing a separation as they argue. In this case, the actors don't have to step back to show distance between themselves. In another example, the camera tracks while the man who found the body enters the room, leading him in a medium shot. When he sees the gun on the bed, the viewer sees it too. Working this tightly, the actor merely has to look at the gun for the viewer to know

Illustration 16

that he has seen it. A "pointing" gesture would be superfluous and, more importantly, would interrupt the action. To work within the frame, actors often have to accomplish contortions that are even more difficult and more illogical than holding a dispassionate conversation at three inches distance. Prop handling may become particularly difficult. A coffee cup that seems comfortably held at bust level will need to be held after each sip just under chin level in order to be used in a shoulder shot, for example *(see illustration 16).*

Having the body adjusted or tilted, the shoulders moved an inch this way or that, the actor may feel like a prop and, inevitably, is a prop, playing to fit the director's composition. Performing for the composition may be something as simple as staying to the left side of the frame on a talk show so that the logo can show up on the right. In a dramatic show, the actor might work with the director and set designer to clearly define the center of interest within the frame. This may mean that, in the example of the long shot of the detective in the doorway, the actor's body and head are part of a design that draws attention to the dead person on the floor. The phone has to be placed to draw imaginary lines that will begin with it and run from left to right, as we read, and flow to the floor. Since diagonal directions in composition have an unbalanced, exciting feeling, compared to the overly stable lines of right angles, the director might ask the detective character to create a diagonal composition by leaning in the frame. In a medium shot, sitting on a chair by the phone, the actor might simply lean forward to change the feel of the scene.

Our eyes only take in about one-twelfth of the screen at once, and a scene with too many areas of attention can irritate or confuse the viewer. Unlike a paiting, which is meant to be studied, the moving image on the screen creates only a fleeting effect. Viewers will grasp some essential information that is focused for them within the frame. For example, they will see the body on the floor but will not count the buttons of the detective's suit.

SCALE OF GESTURE

The gestures that define space or conform to compositional lines can have a scaled-down, "conversational" or natural style. Cutting from a close-up of the face to a detail shot of that person's worried hands has been used as a narrative device since the beginning of film. The hands don't have to be wrung in an exaggerated manner for us to see that the person is upset. In fact, they can be very slightly tensed. And the face could show none of the worry. The purpose of the edit, from face to hands, emphasizes how well the character is hiding his emotion. Natural gestures can be magnified on the screen. They serve to create a character in ways unknown to the stage: biting the nails, for example, or the way a person eats hurriedly or sleeps curled up. Again it is a matter of finding the proper angle from which to shoot these simple acts, to open them up for the viewer. A back can be more expressive than a face—if the character stands up into a high-angle shot and looks down at a frightened child.

If the actor knows how small or how large the scale of a frame is, then his or her position, movement and gestures should seem more natural, even though in reality they may feel very unnatural. The relative size of elements in a frame helps create a mood and direction for a scene—and for a single fleeting frame. This is the power of TV and film: they show us routine events in new ways, from different angles; they get us to notice a telephone or the surface of a desk—things that don't normally stand out in daily life. And the composition of a wide shot can create multiple areas of interest and action: our eyes go from phone to body to detective to body again.

REFERRING BEYOND THE FRAME

While working within the frame, the actor may discover something in the space outside the frame, and may purposefully draw attention to the frame's limits. Such an action may demand a new view and give the viewer a new perspective. A row of jurors, for example, listens to a judge's directions. One is looking away, however. What is that juror looking at? The camera cuts to the defendant, defiantly facing them. All the other jurors are avoiding the defendant's gaze.

Actors will often be asked to refer to the space outside the frame, their motions thus linking them to the unseen situation. This is as true on a talk show, when the host looks over for a guest's entrance, as on the news, when the weatherperson, finishing a report, turns to the sports person, who is in fact across the studio. The cut from one to another binds them together: the performer's look up or to one side takes the place of actual *movement* on the stage.

WORKING WITHIN FRAMES

Actors will generally find it helpful to think of gestures and movement in three categories. First, there are movements that carry the body or a part of the body *beyond* the frame—an entrance or exit, a waving gesture to signal another to enter. Second, there are movements that keep the actor in the frame but change his or her relationship to the edges. Such movements—a leaning left or right, slumping in a chair—are all "in-frame" movements. The third category might be called "in-body" movements. These are small but significant gestures that occur within the space the body occupies; they do not change the actor's relationship to the frame. Such movements as crossing the arms, rubbing the arm, raising the eyebrows or scratching the face are familiar "in-body" gestures. Stage-trained actors often find it extremely difficult to use these small natural movements in a normal or even reduced scale. They are, however, the movements that give density and texture to the actor's image on the screen, the devices that help the actor use the medium to its fullest.

An awareness of these possibilities, combined with an understanding of the relative nature of size and space in the TV image, should help the actor choose the correct gestures and scale them properly. While a frame may at first seem limiting and unnatural to an actor, with experience, he or she will find a whole new range of expression and movement available.

6

EDITING AND THE ACTOR:
Rhythm, Pace and Accent

Time on television is conveyed by the way images and scenes are put together. The flow of the actor's performance is largely controlled by the director and the editor, who make choices about what goes before or after something on the screen. Actors have to work within time frames determined by the editing plan of the script. A scene of child abuse might be intercut with shots of the neighbors arriving and of the police conferring with the neighbors. The abuse scene in real life might take twenty minutes; as an opener on an action series, it could be encapsulated in much less time. The minute or so during which the parent and child are on the screen has to give the feel of the full twenty minutes, even though that minute might be cut into several sets of shots that are to be intercut with the other action.

The director is looking ahead to how the viewer will take in these jigsaw pieces. The actor has to appreciate not only the performance problems of simplified and quick characterization, but also the compositional and narrative problems that the director has to solve. Actors have to understand the vocabulary and conventions of film and TV editing before they can adjust themselves to the particular demands editing can make on their performances.

TIME AND SPACE

Editing organizes time; the duration of shots affects our understanding of space and place. We see a year's events in three minutes, a day's events in three hours. We go from New York to London in a thirtieth of a second; we spend a full minute studying the trip up a staircase from a dozen angles. We move forward and backward from an easily changed present point. A variety of editing conventions is available to the director to express these changes in time, and audiences have become accustomed to them. Conventionally, the *dissolve* from one image to another has been used to indicate a short time lapse, usually less than twenty-four hours. In contrast, when one image *fades out* to black and another image *fades in,* a longer time is understood to have passed. The abrupt *cut* between images signifies no real time break, or a very short one. For example, a director might cut from a character leaving his house to the moment when he boards a bus.

Audio cues are also used to signal changes of time and place. Music or recognizable sounds, such as outside traffic noise or the shouts of school children, will often create new time and place reference and will change the mood between scenes. Faced with the difficulty of identifying points in time, some timid editors have used calendar pages, titles or a prop that abruptly announces another era or a new day. Audiences, however, generally understand and appreciate more subtle cues, and they can wait for the story to unfold. They follow changes in time as easily as they accept entirely original and humanly impossible perspectives on a scene—the view of a room from the chandelier or from the inside of refrigerator when the door opens. The pleasure of the medium is discovered through these rapid changes from below to above, outside to inside, one city to another, now to then.

The director's initial choices about the kind of shots to take determines the possible choices eventually made in the editing room. For example, a worker leaving the factory at the end of the day might be shot in one of two ways. He could be seen in a long shot, his figure dwarfed against the factory wall in the background. Other workers hurry past him, in and out of the frame. Cutting to him, as he pauses for a second, we are prepared to catch the most subtle signs of exhaustion. On the other hand, he might be shot as he moves along, the camera moving with him at his eye level. Such a shot gives an entirely different sense. The worker is no longer dwarfed. As the background changes behind him, he seems to be making progress. The camera slowly drops behind him as he approaches his destination, a bus stop or a corner store, He now seems to have a sense of direction as we see the scene from his point of view. Editing decisions—about how long each shot is held and in what order the shots appear—will change the emphasis of the scene. The statement that the scene makes about the worker, however, is determined by the kind of shots initially taken.

RHYTHM

The performer has to learn to work within the timing established by the planned editing sequence: length, kind and order of the shots. The actor is responsible for creating an overall rhythm that fits both the character and the material, but the presentation of that rhythm will be very different from its presentation on the stage or its occurrence in daily life. The way the scene is shot or edited might create a rhythm, pace (speed), accent or coloration that replaces or even negates the actor's interpretation. Though countless examples are possible, two will suffice. In the first situation below, cutting away to the close-up shot of an object complements the actor's rhythm, slows the pace and accents the scene. In the second, the choice of shots and the speed of cutting sets up a rhythm, pace and accent largely independent of the actors.

> 1. A character crumples a half-written letter and lets it drop to the floor. A *close-up* shot of the letter takes the place of an effort by the actor to portray a moment of intense emotion. The cutting sparks the viewer's imagination instead of milking the actor's expression.
> 2. An argument is occurring between two characters. The scene begins on a *two-shot,* followed by shots cutting between the two actors. As the argument continues, the shots become tighter and tighter *close-ups,* and the cameras are switched between the actors at an increasingly rapid rate. The argument will have a sense of intensity and speed.

As an actor, you need to prepare and understand the overall rhythm of a scene, but you also must be ready to relinquish the expression and interpretation of rhythm to the director. For the actor, it is a matter of trusting the director's judgment when the director says that the cutting will express the importance of the exchange or the sorrow of the moment. The cutting, in fact, allows for more subtle acting, a playing of ambivalences and underplaying of the surface. A heated argument can be played without shouting, sorrow played without sobbing.

TRANSITIONS

The actor is often called on to create special rhythms, generally through gesture, that help blend one cut into another. A news anchor person will look to one side to lead into the cut to a film clip, in a dramatic sequence, an actor may look down and close his or her eyes to end a sequence that fades to black. In numerous similar situations, the actor must adjust performance movements to the cutting rhythm and must anticipate these cuts to facilitate the smooth transitions common to television style. TV programming is designed to fit into the daily household routine. Therefore, the style of programming for TV has been geared to reducing the shocks of transitions inherent in moving pictures. The TV camera operator habitually recomposes the frame, adjusting to every slight movement of the performer, to keep the performer's position in the frame constant. This practice tends to homogenize the feel of the TV picture and make it "soft" and unobtrusive.

Within a given scene, "seamless" transitions are effected by cutting on a movement and following the movement from another viewpoint. For example, in a soap opera, as Maurice enters, Harriet will swivel on her bar stool in a *waist shot* and then hunker down over her drink in a *bust shot* taken from the other side of the bar. The *cut* goes from the *waist shot* to the *bust shot* as she swivels out of one frame and into the other. Cutting from a *close-up* of Harriet to a *close-up* of Maurice is smoothed over by a tilt of her head or a glance of her eyes. Later in the scene, a *medium shot* of Maurice raising a glass to his mouth will be cut to a *shoulder shot*, following the bend of his elbow as the glass comes up.

As you watch TV, notice how standing up and sitting down are handled; watch how and where shots change on movement. Cutting is often smoothed by simple transitional gestures. In a chase, the hunted woman looks over her shoulder; we cut to the posse. Such gestures are often necessary to smooth cutting in current TV, because cuts are usually word to word or person to person. Rarely is atmosphere created by showing a scene before or after the character's dramatic action. In film, a director and editor will create the transition by a shot of the environment or by a bird's-eye view of the scene as the character leaves.

In TV, the transitional gesture is often abstract. One actor has a final gesture that leads into another actor's scene, though the scenes are not necessarily related. The obvious or "formal" connection is similar to the glance of the eyes or the turn of the head used in intercutting conversations. Movements at the end of one scene and the beginning of another seem to relate, even though the scenes have little relationship to each other in terms of content. In film, this technique is known as the *match cut,* and it has been used to link scenes through a similarity in objects or sounds: the wheels of a civilian car dissolve to the wheels of an army jeep; the surf at the beach cuts to the urban sound of distant highway traffic; the bell on the phone changes to the bell in the boxing ring.

ACTOR SKILLS

The transitional gestures characteristic of commercial television are not, of course, the only demands made on the actor for creating rhythm, pace and accent. The actor's own skills in creating variations in timing and emphasis do not go unused. As an actor on TV, you need the skill of the stage performer to create rhythm, pace and accent, but you must also be able to restrain them or even throw them out. Great flexibility is demanded. A stage actor delivering the line, "How dare you?" will accent the word "dare" by lengthening the vowel, by volume, by short beats before and after the word or by "spitting it out." On camera, however, you might be asked to flatten the reading, to underplay it or swallow it because a close-up will carry the emphasis. More complex, complicated emotions can be shown in the close-up—anger mixed with fear or shame, for example. Such conflicting emotions are visible to the viewer on TV, who is able to pick up the most fleeting cues. On stage they would probably be missed.

In another case, the "How dare you?" line might be delivered only as a voice-over, while the shot is focused on the other character's reaction. In this situation, it might be necessary to accent the "dare" to make it stand out. As we explained in Chapter 2, volume would not be a particularly effective option. Instead, a subtle emphasis could be achieved by a vocalized pause, such as an audible breath or a slight choking noise; by squawking out the "d" sound; or by changing to a high pitch on the word. It's possible that, in a voice-over, the "dare" will be emphasized not by your reading but by the other character's physical response. It is even possible that the line might be dropped by the director, allowing the challenge and response to speak silently for itself. The actors would then be responsible for creating much of the rhythm and pace of the scene through appropriate physical gestures.

PACE

In creating the overall timing for a scene, you have to make a distinction between rhythm and pace. A waltz with a flowing rhythm may be fast or slow in pace; a funeral march and a triumphal march have a staccato rhythm but differ in pace. Interesting combinations can be created once an actor can separate his or her rhythm structure from the speed at which the material is performed. A news anchor person, like Cronkite or Walters, talks at as fast a pace as, if not a faster one than, does Carol Burnett. But the variety show seems to go at a breakneck speed and be quite lively as compared to the solidity of the news. This paradox is partially explained by faster cutting and the more varied angles used in the comedy program. The effect, however, is also sustained by the actors, who change rhythms frequently and stop and start unpredictably. The news, on the other hand, uses very regular and predictable rhythms.

In both types of show, neither the rhythm nor pace have much to do with specific content. Burnett and Cronkite seem the same every night, year after year. In general, she reflects entertainment bravado and he, the paternal teacher. Their rhythmic patterns, their simplified catalogue of gestures and verbal mannerisms are memorable long after a particular sketch or a news story has slipped from our minds.

SUMMARY

All performances on TV are finalized in the editing stage and the actor must give up much in terms of controlling his or her rhythm and timing. Performers may not even know in what order their scenes will appear. Understanding the editing plan—when a director chooses to share it—may help a performer in his or her work. In any case, the actor must have sufficient skill to work within the editing requirements, even if these may seem arbitrary and awkward at the moment of shooting. (Motivating technical directions is discussed in Chapter 17.)

7

THE TV STUDIO:
Layout and Equipment

The simplest aspects of TV production could leave a performer indefinitely bemused, but when someone explains the purpose of an interruption in shooting, the function of the person with the clipboard or the destination of a cable that disappears into the wall, many performers feel real relief. If you learn the basic elements of TV production, including the division of labor, protocol and technological requirements, you will feel more at home in any studio, from a network in Los Angeles through a corporate video center to a cable system's small local origination room.

For a formula setup, such as the interview, the panel discussion, or the illustrated lecture, the studio can be astonishingly small, the show being worked with little camera movement, lighting adjustment or performer action. A large-scale production, on the other hand, like the Bunker household set, with several rooms, or a variety special, featuring a line of dancers, can call for a space the size of a basketball court, with almost as much action.

A large setting can be divided to create different environments that are not even physically connected. In a talk show, for instance, a guest may get up to do a song. She walks out of the frame as the host introduces her. We cut to her waiting for us in front of another background that may be on the opposite side of the studio, separated by both crew and equipment that the viewer never sees.

A large studio is an absolute necessity in a live show. It is also economical in videotaping for broadcasting later, because it allows several sets to be used without tearing down between scenes. Both large and small studios will usually be surrounded by a tautly pulled curtain, familiar to stage actors, called a *cyclorama* or *cyc* for short. The cyc provides a neutral, evenly textured background that can serve as the backdrop for an information/news show or as a fill-in around the flats in case the camera operator overshoots the edge of the set. Often the space behind the cyc is used for storage of sets and back-up or special equipment.

Most studios are equipped with at least three cameras. These are generally mounted on *pedestals* or rolling tripods that require a hard, smooth floor surface for dolly or trucking shots.

A microphone *boom* uses a telescopic arm to lower the mike into the set, out of the camera's frame but close to the actors' mouths. The boom operator sits or stands on a rolling platform from which the microphone is panned, tilted, moved in and out. The boom normally remains stationary within each take, and is moved between scenes or adjusted between takes in order to get better sound, to make way for camera movement and to avoid throwing shadows into areas covered by camera shots.

Lighting instruments are hung from a *grid* of pipes suspended about fifteen feet from the floor. Often lights will be suspended from accordionlike supports called *pantographs.* They may also hang on collapsible poles that can be used to adjust their height. In some cases, lights will be used on tripod stands on the floor but, since space is rarely available, the flexibility of such film-style lighting is usually sacrificed to the demands of multi-camera TV studio production. All the lighting instruments are wired to a *dimmer* panel, which is used to turn them on and off and to control their intensity. With current dimmer models, it is possible to pre-set lighting plots, selecting and adjusting a group of lights that can be called up instantaneously on cue at a point in the program. Two sets of lights can be prepared for an area that will serve as the background for a duet as well as a dance number.

The *control room* which is separate from the studio, is where the director works. It houses the *switcher*, the *audio-mix panel* and various operators and assistants. The room is often completely blocked from a direct view of the studio. Instead, the director is able to see what each camera is focused on. A bank of television monitors shows the director the *output* (the picture) on each camera. The *line monitor* shows the signal that is being recorded or transmitted. The audio-mix panel and the switcher or video mixer are, like the dimmer panel, essentially junction boxes. They take inputs from several sources and enable the operator to select and mix them. The audio mixer has inputs from film projectors, videotape decks, audio tape decks and phonographs, as well as from microphones on the floor and from an announcer who is often in a separate booth or at a table on the floor.

The audio-mix panel is often in a separate room so that the sound recordist can concentrate on audio quality without the distracting activity of the control booth. The switcher, or *special-effects generator* (SEG), takes the inputs of studio and remote cameras, videotape recorders (VTR), film and 35mm slide projectors and word- or character-generators. The switcher can cut the screen into an endless variety of shapes and feed video signals to fit them.

The *split screen* is the simplest example. One camera can have a waist shot of a news anchor person on the right side of the frame. That shot can be mixed with the left side of location footage—a picket line, for example—played back as the anchor person introduces that story. The switcher can cut to a full shot of the picket line, or a shot of the anchor person, or use a *wipe* effect that seems to push and image off the screen until only one figure remains. The switcher can also *fade out* and *fade in* from a picture, *dissolve* or *superimpose* one signal over another at any degree of intensity.

A close shot of one dancer can be *superimposed* over a wider shot of a group of dancers. The close shot could be used as a pale shape, or it could be balanced in intensity with the wider shot.

In color television, *keying* allows for a more controlled and very useful effect, similar to the matte shots of film. One signal is cut into another. You see it most often on the news: Walter Cronkite sitting in front of a picture illustrating his story. Actually, he is sitting in front of a colored rectangle. The illustration is a slide on a slide projector, which is operated in a film chain that is connected to a video camera, which in turn feeds a signal into the switcher. The operator, using the switcher, or *special-effects generator,* selects a color, usually green or blue, that will be filled in by the inserted source. The second source is keyed to the hue and will take over the signal wherever the color occurs. Thus, the body of an actor dressed in a blue suit in a blue chroma key set will disappear along with the blue background. These effects, useful for fantasy, have been widely exploited in advertising. In some commercials, actors are required to move through a blue background and floor onto which another scene has been inserted. An actor can appear to be standing beside a gigantic bottle of detergent which actually is an ordinary ten-inch bottle shot in close-up and keyed into an empty blue setting.

The people in the control room are connected to the studio personnel by an *intercom system.* Camera and boom operators wear headsets wired to the control room; they follow commands or respond to the director through the headsets. The *floor manager* often uses a wireless headset with a portable transmitter, which provides maximum mobility. The director also has a *studio announce* (SA), or studio talkback public address system, which allows amplified communication to everyone in the studio at once. Additionally, there are monitors in the studio itself that show the *line* (what is actually being transmitted) for the benefit of the crew and talent.

The *master control room* houses the videotape recorders, camera control units and the equipment for processing (strengthening, shaping) and measuring the electronic signal. The *cine-chain,* or film chain, is also set up and operated from master control. The purpose of the film chain is simple; non-studio input can be mixed with studio input through the switcher. The chain connects a 16mm film, or 35mm slide, for example, to another TV camera, whose output is registered in the control room. A film clip from a movie appearing during a Johnny Carson interview or a slide of a logo for station identification are two instances where a film chain is used.

Frequently there is also a *character-generator* in master control. Essentially a computerized typewriter with memory storage, it is used to display words over a picture (e.g., a title, credits or someone's name). A character-generator ordinarily has a selection of type faces and sizes. Credits at the end of a show are typed on a character-generator and are rolled out at a choice of speeds over whatever other visual inputs the director chooses.

The form of the studio may vary, but the elements composing any studio are fairly standard. In small shops, the control booth, audio booth and master control often share the same space. In a large station, the control room, master control and the stage may be separated by miles of corridor. Regardless of where people or equipment are located, the actor must be oriented to each production component.

8

DIVISION OF LABOR:
Roles and Responsibilities

In TV production work, so many components make up a single production that an extensive division of labor is necessary. An evening news show can have fifty credits. But in small studios you might be working with only a handful of people: a camera operator who does the lighting, a producer who does the casting and makes the calls for lunch and so on. In a single-camera production, you might work with a crew of only three: director, camera and audio, with all three working on lighting.

If you understand the elements of production as you understand the studio layout, and if you grasp the detailed division of labor, you can adjust to any situation: those where responsibilities are minutely divided, where they are shared or where they are hyphenated, and one person is writer–director–producer, or set-designer–makeup-artist–property manager. If, for example, a small studio operates without an individual floor manager, you should understand the role of a floor manager enough to be able to see who is doing those tasks. It is usually a camera operator or a production assistant.

In broadcast TV, there is a fairly rigid division of labor in the major markets at most stations, a division that is specified by union contracts negotiated by each local. These agreements define scheduling and jurisdiction over equipment with firm rules about when you eat and when you take a break, who can copy a tape or touch a camera. As video takes the place of film, with attendant union battles over jurisdiction and with wider distribution of programming through videodiscs, cassettes and pay-cable, many innovations in the modes of production are expected even at the broadcast level.

The technical crew includes camera operators, sound recordists, switcher, engineers, lighting director and floor manager and the "creative" artists and management include writer, producer, director, various associates and assistants and talent, which includes actors, performers and animals.

Typically, you will find half a dozen workers on the studio floor. Each one has a specific task that is crucial to the total production. Knowing the responsibilities of each prevents misunderstandings and confusion.

The *microphone-boom operator* knows the format or script as thoroughly as anyone. The boom ducks down into close shots, but must tilt up and telescope back for wide shots. The boom operator understands the blocking of the actors of performers and follows their action with the microphone, anticipating their delivery.

The *floor manager* (FM) is responsible for all the studio traffic of people and gear and relates commands from the control room to the talent. The floor manager tells the talent when to start and stop, adjusts blocking, reminds performers of their marks and gets them into position for rehearsals and retakes *(see illustration 17)*. Everyone on the floor reports to the floor manager, who schedules breaks and reconvenes cast and crew. Stage hands and an assistant work under the floor manager to put sets up and furniture in place. Additionally, the floor manager is often involved in pre-production planning.

The *camera operator* manipulates the position of the camera and lens. Camera operators use *shot sheets* which, in a completely scripted show, will tell them exactly where to be, when and with what kind of shot.

While the camera operator finds the shot, focuses the camera, raises or lowers the pedestal and prepares a pan or a dolly, the *engineer* in master control sets up and monitors the resolution, the color and the lights and darks of the picture. These adjustments are made to the signal from the camera control unit to the camera via cable. The engineer works closely with the lighting director, set designer and camera operators, since work done in each area introduces variables into the image quality. Color or gray-scale tonal quality and the emphasis of highlights are largely controlled by the engineer, who equalizes all camera input and who creates the mood demanded by both script and direction.

In the control booth, the *technical director* (TD) operates the switcher to take line (on-air) and preview (off-air) shots and to set up effects. The TD takes cues from the associate director "for preview," or what is *prepared* for broadcast. The director gives the TD *ready cues*—"Ready camera 1"—then *take cues*—"Take camera 1."

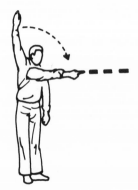

Stand by; go ahead.

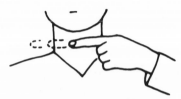

Cut it; stop; finish; omit rest of item.

You are cleared. You are now off camera and can move, or stop action.

Slow down; slower pace; stretch it out. (Indicated by slow "stretching" gesture.)

You're on that camera, play to that camera. (Sometimes preceded by "Turning actor's head" gesture.)

Volume up; louder.

Speed up; faster pace; quicker tempo. (Movement's speed shows amount of increase.)

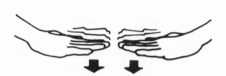

Volume down; quieter (sometimes precede by "Quiet" signal).

Wind-up now.

Illustration 17

The *audio-mixer* or *sound operator,* is often stationed in a separate part of the control room or in a separate area near the control room. Microphones, audio tape decks, film sound, turntables and sound from videotape decks are all sources that feed into an audio-mix panel. At the mixer they are combined, controlled for volume and quality and selected for "line out" to be recorded or transmitted with the "line-out" video signal.

The audio mixer is responsible for microphone selection and placement. Like the camera operator in a complex show, where several inputs are used, the audio mixer has to have a shot sheet to prepare switches to new mikes and sources. The *associate director* (AD) should ready the mixer, telling him or her to stand by. The director will call for new sources, such as music or film sound. Nevertheless, the mixer is responsible for following the audio of the program and anticipating the script.

The *director* is responsible for the artistic quality of the program, its visual composition and rhythm and the emphases controlled by lighting, audio and stage design. He or she must be able to make demands on all the technical skills assembled to create the show—to ask for something from a performer or a lighting director or a makeup artist that will fit the script or enhance the show's look. Directors must understand the craft vocabulary of all the technicians and be able to schedule rehearsals and arrange tasks in order of importance.

There is never enough time to solve every problem or to get the most out of every crew and cast member. That is why the most successful TV directors are those who are able to pre-plan effectively and who use their associate director and floor manager to extend their influence on the cast and crew.

The *Associate Director's* (AD) job is to prepare the shots on camera so that the director will be able to make fine adjustments without dealing with gross traffic and framing. The AD makes sure that the camera operator is following the shot sheet and is at the next mark. For example, the AD may say, "Camera 2 coming up to shot 86, a close-up of Amy, focus up 2." If that is the next shot, the AD will say "Preview 2" to the technical director. The director will then have a few final decisions to make and may correct framing, saying for instance, "Tilt up a little Camera 2, lose her shoulder; tighten up, lose the hair."

Or the director may tell Camera 2 to pan left a little to see something in the background to match the cut with the camera currently on line. Listening to the verbal cues, the director will call for the shot at the right moment, at the same time that the AD is looking ahead to the setup of shots by the camera not on line or preview. As soon as the preview is taken, the AD begins again to set up the camera that is just "off line."

Associates are often chosen to round out the deficiencies of the director or producer. Outside of the control booth, the AD's role isn't fixed. One director might use an AD to calm and prepare performers, another, to work with camera placement on the floor and focal-length selection.

The *producer* is often the key figure in commercial television, carrying a project through from the idea stage to pre-production writing, set design and casting. The producer may work with the director on the actual production to integrate budget and scheduling demands. The producer may also carry through to post-production involvement with the editor, composer, credit designer and so on. Directors rarely play the kind of ongoing role in the development of a series that is typical of a producer.

There is a widespread popular image of the producer as a short fat money man with a cigar and the director as the creative force battling for the integrity of his or her art. This image has its roots in film and stage, where it is of course less than true, but you would be even more lost if you carried this cliche into television work. In most cases it is the producer who has developed the overall concept for the show and who maintains aesthetic control. The director is often brought in very late in studio productions and has the job of translating the producer's ideas into the possibilities of production, acting more like a director of photography in film than the auteur.

Most above- (creative) and below-the-line (technical) personnel work with clearly defined job patterns, but they may have to adjust to meet actual production circumstances. Once the basic job patterns are known, a performer can more easily work with whatever variations or unusual circumstances develop in production. If the actor is pleasant and responsive, studio and technical personnel are usually cooperative and patient. Experience and confidence with the medium increases the performer's ease in the working situation.

9

SHOOTING:
Multi-Camera, Single-Camera,
Studio and Location

There are many different ways to record a performance. The original distinctions between TV and movie shooting techniques have been blurred by technical innovations and market demands. Traditionally, film technique has meant working with a single camera, stopping and starting, shooting out of the sequence in short bits, with repeated takes, the final product actually being created in editing. Television technique has meant working with three or four cameras in a single take and recording or transmitting live.

In the TV drama of the fifties, multi-camera live transmission demanded a near-military meticulousness, with constant compromises in all aspects of production. At its best, the live drama fit the limitations of TV production because it was structured in long scenes and in real time. In some cases, complicated effects of setting and mood were achieved by careful pre-production planning for sound mix and camera work. However, live TV's strengths have really been more fully revealed in coverage of spontaneous events, such as talk shows, congressional hearings and football games. In any one of these shows, a director makes hundreds of editing decisions in a single program.

One-take, live TV means the instant cut, the push of the button that switches the viewers from one frame to another. Film-style shooting for television means the building of a program through take after take, shot after shot. This approach allows attention to be given to detail of performance and production values that obviously is not possible in live TV, no matter how thoroughly the live show is rehearsed. These distinctions between film and TV shooting are useful for setting a frame of reference, although they do not actually reflect the full range of current video production practice. The purpose of this chapter is to survey contemporary shooting styles as they affect the performer, with specific suggestions for coping with various working situations.

MULTI-CAMERA PRODUCTION

In Chapter 2 we mentioned the invention of multi-camera filming before a live audience for the *I Love Lucy Show*. Multi-camera filming had been used early in the movies to save time and to guarantee coverage of an action without having to set up the same action again in order to record another angle. A man leaving his car and crossing the street puts on his hat. We cut to a reverse angle to see where he's going. Shooting single camera, the director and actor have to think about *continuity* problems. At what point in crossing the street does he put on the hat, and how does he put on the hat? The motion has to be repeated some time later, after the crew has moved across the street and set up to shoot the reverse angle. If he puts on the hat with the wrong hand or halfway across the street instead of two-thirds across, then there will be a jump in the editing from hand to hand, or of his body's position in relation to background cues.

With two cameras and two crews, both angles are recorded at once, and the matching is guaranteed. But the specific problem of acting for the cut is added to the situation. If the actor knows that a cut is intended at that point, then he has to be clear with the director about performance size and gesture in relation to lens focal length, depth of field and lighting. The advantage of single camera shooting for the actor is that these questions can be considered and tackled shot by shot. The disadvantage lies in the difficulty of creating a unified performance.

For TV, the use of multi-camera technique to film *I Love Lucy* not only gave a means of preserving the image, but also allowed fine editing decisions to be made later in the film-cutting room instead of under the pressure of the TV control room. The introduction of videotape and electronic videotape editing made it possible for the same technique to be used on video. Shooting with several cameras at once can mean that the director is choosing editing points as the action progresses, and recording one version of the performance. It can also mean that, while the director is calling a primary version of sequence of shots, other cameras are also being recorded for post-production editing. With videotape, there is now a tendency to record the signals of all cameras, or of at least two cameras, to enable a selection of shots to be made after the performance or show.

The major difference in TV production styles is not so much

between film and tape, but between *short-take* and *long-take* styles. *The Mary Tyler Moore Show* was filmed in the multi-camera style. It was edited afterwards—with several hundred edits per show—but it was shot in long scenes in front of a live audience. In single-camera shooting, a simple set of shots (such as Mary at her desk looking up at Lou's entrance and saying, "Mr. Grant," and then Lou entering and saying "Mary," and their subsequent conversation) would each be done separately. There would be a shoulder shot of Mary at her desk, followed by a waist shot of Lou, with the remainder of the conversation contained in a two-shot. With the multi-camera technique, three film cameras could shoot the whole scene at the same time, and the scene would then be cut together later, without wasting the time and energy consumed by setting up three shots.

In *The Mary Tyler Moore Show*, this short exchange was part of a long, commercial-to-commercial scene that included the entrances and exits of several other characters. Many broadcast shows are now being shot on videotape, recording the output of all the cameras, but shooting such short exchanges without a live audience. The advantage lies in being able to pursue a shot, or a short sequence of shots, through several takes until the director is satisfied, something that cannot be done with a live audience.

All in the Family was shot on videotape twice in the same night and edited together from both tapings. It was, however, very similar to the filmed *Mary Tyler Moore Show* in pace and cuts and in its demands on the actors, both shows being shot in long takes, before a studio audience, using a frontal stage. *All in the Family* was recorded from commercial to commercial, straight through. The director used four cameras, with three of them always recording. The actors knew which particular shot was primary and play for that specified camera. At the same time, the actors had to be aware that the two other shots were being recorded on other equipment decks as back-up choices, to catch reactions and wider shots and to allow for adjustments in timing. These other recording decks are called *ISO* (isolated) decks, and there is either an ISO director or an assistant director who makes the calls for the back-up material. In using an ISO deck, the director is still trying to call a complete show. In *All in the Family*, after performing for their first audience each time, the cast and director would review the show, plan any changes and try it again for a second audience. The final program for broadcast was then edited from the less-than-three-hours of video tape recorded during the two playings. The first taping was called a dress rehearsal, but often more of that performance was used for broadcast than the material from the second taping.

In a contrasting example, *Barney Miller* is shot on videotape, without an audience, with four cameras recording each short scene. The director works on a sequence again and again, completes it and goes on to the next. The actors are blocked for the action and are not playing to one particular camera. In editing, there are forty hours of tape to choose from, to put together one half-hour show. A fifth camera and deck is used to record the bank of monitors that show the output of the four cameras on the floor. The tape from the fifth recorder is used to view the alternative shots side by side during editing.

CAMERA BLOCKING

No matter what the production style, the talent/actors are not necessarily always blocked for the camera. Instead, they can be blocked in relation to each other, to properties, to settings. Even in the early days of live TV drama there were programs that used improvisation both by the actors and by the director calling the shots. *Studs' Place* (1950–1951) was broadcast for two years live from Chicago, with Studs Terkel playing a bar owner. The regular cast of characters improvised dialogue and action from a script outline. It is, in fact, possible to shoot a somewhat open-ended show like this if it is highly formated, with a set series of shots dictated by the setting and the gestural characterization of the actors. A football game is quite similar. There is a stock vocabulary of shots; choices have to be made during the action, but within narrow alternatives.

In a formated show, such as an interview or game show, each camera has a given area of coverage. In an interview, for example, one camera might be told to cover the interviewer with a close-up, an over-the-shoulder two shot or a wide shot of the whole studio for transitions, such as entrances and the "in-and-out" of commercial breaks. In this case, the director will talk to each operator individually in order to set up a change in shots and allow time for him to get the new shot while another camera is on line. This kind of area coverage allows the director to plan categories of shots; it also allows for the rapid switching between cameras that gives the show its density.

A guest on a talk show will simply be told where to sit. The chair has been blocked, not the talent; it is placed to give the optimum shots. Usually this shooting approach involves cross-shooting the host and guest, as they look toward each other, their bodies slightly angled out to open themselves up to the cameras. This shot allows for a simple cutting back and forth between static cameras, while giving an acceptable variety of shots. The director can also open up the profiles of the talent by changing the camera positions during the interview, by varying the shot sizes and by using simple frame movement, like the *dolly* or the *zoom*.

Performer movement can enhance this shooting setup enormously. A natural turning away from your partner's eye contact to pause, to show you're thinking, to begin to answer a question before you turn back—these gestures open up your full face to the camera, give a sense of your wholeness and create activity in the frame that punctuates the audio. The talk show guest, the news anchor person, the reviewer or consumer affairs reporter—all succeed when they allow the camera to see them fully, to see their hesitations, their thoughtfulness, their work at their papers, their bodies shifting position—all as a way of indicating thought.

The openings and closings of these partially scripted shows are usually blocked carefully. The host of an interview might introduce the program by talking directly into a specified camera lens and then turning to the guest and engaging in lively reaction and gesture. The opening shot size and camera is planned, but from then on—until the close or transitions to commercials—the host should concentrate on the guest and let the director capture their "actuality" together. Many of their reactions will be lost to the TV audience, yet each reaction is important, for it motivates the guest and gives a wholeness to the performance. Red *tally* lights on the top of the cameras, flashing on and off, will let you know which camera is on-line, but not whether the image is a wide shot or a close-up. An expressive shake of the hand could be lost out of the frame. The perceptive talent may be able to tell from the position of the camera what kind of shot it is getting—whether it's full face, three-quarters or full profile. In a formated talk show, the floor manager's role during taping is simply to cue the opening, close and transitions for the host. The host can see the FM giving a stand-by cue, pointing to the camera for direct presentation and counting off the seconds at each end.

Many directors will block for action in dramatic scenes, especially when shooting short sequences multi-camera and multi-deck. Even in a commercial such as a *Slice-and-Dice* demonstration, the director can plan the shots around the performer's action. You won't worry which camera has a close-up of your hand with the potato peeler, or about the medium shot of you and the table. The action of peeling, your floor marks, the reduced scale of your movement and the size of the table—all restrict you to the frame. There is in fact some leeway in matching shots when recording on more than one deck. For example, the actor who is supposed to turn his or her head as the transition movement from a two-shot to a close-up can miss the cue and turn a little late; the scene can still be edited at the point of the turn, since the master shot, or the cover shot, includes all the action of the scene from one viewpoint. The other shots—close-ups, reactions, details—can be inserted later.

Being blocked to turn on a line of dialogue, or on a specific audio cue, doesn't leave the performer much room for error. A skilled performer will be able to make specific directions work smoothly in complicated multi-camera taping. At a certain point in the *Slice-and-Dice* dialogue, for example, you might be told to lift the peeler to the side of your face and turn to another camera for the final close-up. Awkwardly done, this can appear as if you are looking for the other camera. Correctly done, it will seem to be a natural action, a turning toward the viewers, to show them yourself and the object.

Multi-camera taping puts great demands on the actor to create a continuous performance, while still having to open up to one camera or another. As we have illustrated, inches are critical: the tilt of a head can throw the composition off in a carefully blocked over-the-shoulder shot; a slight movement can drop your mouth out of frame in an extreme close-up. In television, where we're dealing with so many close shots of bodies that fill the frame, the slightest emphasis of body position, the incline of a shoulder or thrust of a hip, can create a frame different from what the director intended. Being blocked for the camera can mean getting directions as precise as moving an inch. It can also mean simply turning from one camera to another, or hitting toe marks of chalk or tape on the studio floor.

Newscasters, who are rarely trained actors, have learned to use their papers as props. They have a simple repertory of pauses, glances down and turns of the body to cover the camera cuts. A story of unemployment will end with a quick glance down at the papers—perhaps shuffling them, making a mark with a pen—and a look up at another camera, making another shot as a lead into another story. The talent is providing the material; it is up to the director to choose the exact moment for the switch to occur in this live format.

Typically, the news anchor person will be sitting in a medium shot with a close-up still photo of the President chroma-keyed or projected at his side. He will turn to say, "Elsewhere in the news," and the director will cut to a waist shot—losing the illustration—with the anchor filling the screen. The newscaster's script is usually marked for camera cuts, and the performer knows which camera is on line.

DRAMATIC BLOCKING

Blocking in a dramatic show will usually make shot-by-shot demands on the actors. To illustrate the requirements of precision performing for the camera, let us consider a simple soap opera scene. We fade up on Harriet at her desk writing a letter. She hears Maurice's voice out-of-frame (OOF) and looks up. Maurice enters her room. She says, "I told you not to come here anymore," gets up, walks around to the front of her desk, and leans against it. Maurice says, "Please, Harriet." She straightens herself and replies, "Maurice, I'll tell you again, it won't work." He takes a step toward her and says, "It's not fair, Harriet." She turns away from him, and we fade to black.

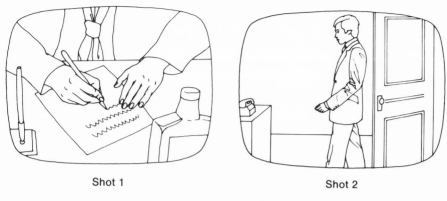

Shot 1   Shot 2

Illustration 18

There are many ways to shoot this scene. We are going to construct it in one take containing seven shots with a three-camera system. The diagram is a common operational sketch that a director might make in thinking through the scene. It shows camera positions and actor positions; the storyboard frames show the relative size of the characters and the use of properties (*see illustration 18*).

Shot #1 is a close-up of Harriet's hand and the letter. The camera is at a high angle to show the top of the desk. It zooms back and tilts up simultaneously to a medium shot of her. She hears Maurice's voice and looks up. The hand and the paper have to fill the frame. The angle of the wrist, the speed of the writing, the pauses in the writing can all change the effect of the first part of the shot.

For the zoom out, Harriet has to be hunched over the desk to fill the medium shot without forcing it to widen to take in her height. The limitation of TV's aspect ratio is illustrated here. The 4 by 3 scale lends itself to lateral movement, not vertical. In any case, no matter how Harriet has been blocked, ramrod straight or collapsed, she has to be there for the camera operator, who has rehearsed a precise zoom and tilt. She also has to be there for the lighting. With her head bent too far in the opening shot, she will cast a shadow on the letter, if she does not lean back far enough for the reaction, he hair might throw a shadow on her face.

In the third part of the shot, Harriet has to raise her head (without anticipating Maurice's entrance) high enough to show her facial response to his voice. At that high angle, she could easily glance up without opening to the camera. If she sits up too far, however, her eyes will go out of the frame. As she looks up, we cut to shot #2, cutting on the movement.

Maurice comes through the door in a knee shot, leaving it open, and

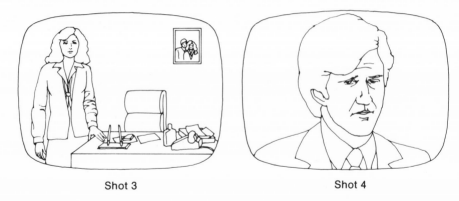

Shot 3   Shot 4

the camera pans with him, leading him, so that the distance between the edge of the frame and his nose stays the same. This move has also been rehearsed; the camera operator is expecting Maurice to move at their rehearsed walking speed, generally slower and with smaller steps than non-screen action.

Maurice also has to hit his toe mark. A key light is waiting for him. If Maurice misses his mark, he may be lit by fill light only, and his face will not have detailed modelling. It will be distractingly different from Harriet's face. As he hits his mark, Maurice looks down, then up at her, holding his breath, then letting it out. His hesitation, his opened lips, almost speaking, is the cue for the cut to shot #3.

Harriet reacts to his timidity, shaking her head in a wide shot. She stands and walks around the side of the desk and leans against it to deliver her line. The boom mike is waiting for her. If she speaks too early, the mike won't be close enough to pick her voice up adequately. If she walks too wide, away from the desk, she might throw the shot off, because the director is working with background and foreground objects that must be given their place in the frame in all these shots. As Harriet walks around the desk to the left of the frame, perhaps we see a framed photo of both characters on the wall in the right of the frame. If Harriet walks too wide to her right, frame left, we lose the picture. If she leans against the desk too far to frame right, she will block the picture, as the camera tightens on her for the line, framing her in a waist shot against the desk.

In the first shot we could see a bottle of brandy in the foreground; if the paper and her hand are moved, the brandy may block them. If the camera trucks right or left to recompose the objects, it may not be set up for the tilt and zoom-out.

In shot #4, camera 1 has a close shoulder shot of Maurice. The actor can make a slight lateral movement, a slump of one shoulder, a cant of

Shot 5   Shot 6

the head. He can lean forward, toward her, as he says, "Please, Harriet." But he cannot bob and weave in the frame; his gestures have to be small, and his hands won't show unless he touches his face. Hand gestures out of the frame might wiggle his shoulders oddly, and his flying fingers might creep up into the bottom of the frame. He has to wait for the boom mike to cue around to him. If he overlaps her line, he won't be on mike. In shot #4 Maurice has to play to Harriet and the camera. This might mean looking at her right cheek instead of her left, in order not to close himself off.

The next shot, as she takes a step toward him and says, "Maurice, I'll tell you again, it won't work," is more difficult. This is a long over-the-shoulder two-shot. The variations are subtle: mere inches of shoulder can fill the frame. A shift of weight off the mark can end up cutting Harriet's face in half and blowing the take. Harriet has to take her step forward just as carefully. If she moves to the left, she'll bury herself behind his shoulder; if she moves to the right she'll lose his shoulder entirely, and the shot will not serve its intention of connecting the characters while setting up the following two-shot. To hit their marks, the actors have established their stride during rehearsal and actually counted the steps. With practice this movement is internalized; the marks are there only to be checked between the takes.

In shot #5, the characters are facing each other frontally. In shot #6, they open up to camera 3 for a two-shot that will give three-quarters of their faces. The boom mike with a cardioid pickup pattern could cover both of them in the open two-shot. Harriet turns to her left, away from Maurice, opening to camera 3 and drawing interest to frame left, preparation for the cut to camera 1. Maurice takes a step toward her to move into the two-shot. If he gets too close, he might obstruct her key light and throw a heavy shadow across her chest.

For shot #7, she recoils and turns completely away from him,

Shot 7

opening a full-face view of her in a shoulder shot enlarged in the foreground, with Maurice behind her in a knee shot. The doorway stands open in the background between them. Harriet has to be aware that the wide angle and her closeness to the lens exaggerates each of her movements. A stillness from Harriet, in contrast to Maurice's fidgeting in the background, would be effective. Both actors have to watch their marks in order to leave the doorway between them. As she turns out of the two-shot, he will turn slightly, following her with his stationary body to help recompose for this foreground-background shot.

In the Harriet-and-Maurice example, the actors have had to be aware of the shots and have had to relate their lines and movement to each camera position and focal length, as well as the boom microphone and the lighting. There is a story about one actor that illustrates a competent TV actor's understanding of shot requirements. In a one-take taped program set in a bar, an actress playing a waitress missed her mark and got between the actor and the camera that was supposed to get his close-up. He ducked down under her arm and around her side, straightened his neck and delivered the line at the same time the camera operator tilted down to catch the shot. This is a definite illustration of an actor working with technicians to make frames, following the pressure to get the lines delivered to the right camera.

In the film-style, multi-camera taping, this short scene with the waitress could have been recorded as a sequence of half a dozen shots, like the Harriet-Maurice scene, and the blocking could have been shot in several takes until it was executed perfectly. However, the show would not necessarily be better for it, since the live-style taping has the energy of a continuous theatre performance.

REMOTE AND SINGLE-CAMERA PRODUCTION

The multi-camera video system can be packaged into vans and taken on location; as the equipment develops and gets smaller, this flexibility will become more commonplace. Currently it is more likely that remote work will be shot with a single-camera system. For the actor, the remote demands extra patience, with the technical problems of weather and noise, scarcity in facilities, and breakdowns in communication between the location and the production house.

Single-camera shooting involves a discontinuity of performance that is difficult for the actor. Time and budget constraints force productions to avoid long chronological sequences. Two scenes in the living room may be shot back-to-back as one equipment setup, with the same camera angle and the same lighting. A scene on the front porch that comes between them in the final edit will be shot later that day as a separate setup, using natural light, waiting for the clouds to go back over the sun or vice versa, reshooting because a plane went by.

A continuity person, or a production assistant, will usually help the actor keep props and body positions straight when there are several setups for different camera angles and lighting changes within one scene, helping him or her remember which hand the cigarette was in, what level the wine was in the glass. In most film-style shooting, the director will plan a master shot in which all the others are contained, and then go in to get close-ups and details. In a wide or long shot, the details of props and clothing are not critical. But in a close shot, the position of the face in the screen is critical. In mid-level shots, it is necessary to watch arm and head positions carefully. In intercutting close shots and two-shots, the performer must take careful note of slight gestures, nods, the hand tugging the ear, the turn of the shoulder.

Continuity also involves the problem of keeping the performers on the same side of the frame before and after a cut. This problem is called crossing the center line or *axis*. In the diagram (*see illustration 19*) you can see that cameras on the same side of a line drawn between two characters will keep them on the same side of the frame. But a camera shot from across that line reverses them and will create a jump effect which is very disconcerting for the audience. This problem also occurs in multi-camera shooting, but the instant comparison of camera monitors reminds the director that the cameras have to be moved back across the line. The line can be crossed by the actor moving, the camera moving or by a narrow lens that catches a close shot without relating it to the background in a way that indicates the change of axis. In leaving one frame and entering the other, the actor has to be shot without crossing the axis, for example, leaving one frame on the left in a medium shot and entering another on the right in a wide shot.

Illustration 19

Cutting from frame to frame also demands a continuity of dialogue to be matched with the action. If an actor waves his hand in a close-up while saying, "Hello, Charlie," and then drops his hand to his side before calling out, "How are you?" he must coordinate the movement and dialogue in *exactly* the same way in a wide shot of the action. Unless he does so, the two angles could not be edited together smoothly.

SUMMARY

Production situations vary considerably. The performer must stay flexible and adjust to the particular demands set up by the style of shooting. The examples discussed here give you some idea of the range of requirements imposed by various approaches to blocking, shot plans and styles of shooting. The performer is central to the video image; the design and flow of any production is inextricably bound up in the skills and timing of the actor. Careful coordination with the wishes of the director and with the production efforts of the crew will help the performer be effective in the frame as well as creative in performance.

Part Two

PREPARING THE PERFORMER AND THE PERFORMANCE FOR TV

10

THE PHYSICAL IMAGE:
The Performer's Visual Effect

Concern about the physical image, the effect one's body has on others, is common to our society. Individuals struggle to achieve certain images, to avoid others in the belief that people will define and evaluate them by the way they look. The "bull-headed" businessman, the "willowy" dancer, the "broad-shouldered" athlete are images that create expectations about behavior and attitudes. While many people may be unnecessarily concerned about their images, TV performers must pay extremely close attention to their physical appearance for three reasons. First, all video work employs close-up camera techniques that reveal the performer's body as if it were under a microscope. Every gesture, every movement, every mole, hair and wrinkle is available to the viewer. Second, TV time is a one-minute or even one-second interval; a viewer's first impression of a performer may well be his or her only impression. Third, in many cases a performer will be hired or not hired because of his or her physical type.

A clearly defined image is necessary every given moment. Commercial work offers an excellent example of the problems involved. In a thirty-second commercial for "over-the-calf" socks, a male performer is asked to appear as a young business executive who is dressing for an important conference and who knows that his boss must be impressed by his appearance. He must convince the viewer 1) that he is a business executive; 2) that a boss will pay attention to appearance; 3) that he believes the "over-the-calf" socks look best; 4) that the viewer needs "over-the-calf" socks. The viewer must believe in the authenticity of the performer for these things to happen. The performer may be on the screen only fifteen seconds; the socks get the rest of the time. One of the major factors creating or detroying the credibility in this piece will be the physical image of the actor.

The ability to control your image, to play the business executive or the grocery store clerk, to be the newscaster or to host the talk show, is a major performance skill. Chapters 10 through 15 are designed to explain problems and techniques related to image and to the creation of image with characters and personalities. The first step in such work, whether one is preparing to perform in a commercial, soap opera or news show, is a clear picture of the physical self. The purpose of this chapter is to present techniques for developing such a picture.

It is usually a difficult and fairly time-consuming task to discover a clear self-image. While most people become aware at a relatively young age that they are seen differently by others than they see themselves, rarely are these differences explored. Preoccupation with fashionable images of the day often blocks self-perception. We search for the "flattering" photograph, the one that corresponds to the magazine image of attractiveness, without recognizing the uniqueness and truth of the "unflattering" one. In a medium as revealing as TV, the only person who does not really see a performer's body often is the performer. Below are techniques that should provide a performer with a clearly developed sense of his or her physical image. Once an image is known, it can, of course, be changed, manipulated and appropriately used.

EXERCISE I

Facing a full-length mirror, begin at the top of your head and describe exactly what you see in your own body. For example, "I have short, straight brown hair that curls slightly over my ears. My ears have large lobes and protrude slightly. My cheeks are fat and rosy." The description should be as objective as possible. You continue through the entire body.

The next step is to list what you most noticed about yourself—three or four prominent features (*e.g.*, fat cheeks, small nose, long arms). Note also those characteristics that you most like and those that you least like.

Third, write a description of yourself as if you were writing a casting information sheet. "John Stevens is a six-foot, two-inch tall Caucasian. He is lanky and thin, with straight collar-length brown hair. He has a sharp chin, high forehead and deep set-eyes. His arms are particularly long. He might be a basketball player or a dancer."

EXERCISE II

Repeat the process in the first exercise with a photograph or a video image of yourself. Note the differences between the real-life description and this one. Cameras do affect appearance. Too, performers are more distant from themselves when observing an image and are more objective in what they see.

EXERCISE III

If possible, ask a professional acquaintance to describe you in the same manner used in Exercise I. This person should also describe the photograph or electronic image used in Exercise II. The differences between how performers see themselves and how others see them is, of course, critical. Note the discrepancies; there are usually a number of differences. Also, ask what features the other person finds most noticeable.

As a second step, try to discover what people see as your most prominent physical characteristics; what are your most and least attractive and/or interesting physical traits. This exercise is most easily done in an acting class or with a group of actors.

EXERCISE IV

From the information you have from Exercises I, II and III, prepare a description of your physical image with the following chart.

1. Age range (18–25, 30–45, etc.)
2. Facial characteristics:
   a. Shape (round, oval, etc.)
   b. Forehead (high, low, prominent, etc.)
   c. Cheeks (full, hollow, etc.)
   d. Eyes (color, shape, size)
   e. Nose (long, small, flat, etc.)
   f. Scars or lines (smile lines, etc.)
   g. Eyebrows (heavy, thin, pale, etc.)
   h. Other (set jaw, etc.)
3. Body type (plump, linear, square, etc.)
4. Posture (erect, stiff, slumped, high shoulders, etc.)
5. Peculiar characteristics (long arms, short neck, etc.)
6. Best or most interesting feature (*e.g.,* high forehead)
7. Worst or least attractive feature (*e.g.,* slumped shoulders)
8. Characteristic most often noticed (*e.g.,* big eyes)

Such an inventory should give a performer a reasonably objective view of his or her physical body. It is, however, a view of a static body; the physical image in video is, of course, a dynamic one. Therefore, in order to complete an inventory of the image, it is important to study *mannerisms* and *movement* as well as appearance.

Because of the close-up style of most video, mannerisms are highly visible, attract attention and make strong statements. On stage, a hand movement, flicker of the eyes or raised eyebrow will rarely be seen. In video, it will always be seen if it is in the shot. You should become aware of such mannerisms as bobbing your head, raising your eyebrows frequently, frowning when thinking, using large and frequent hand gestures to punctuate statements, smiling frequently, unconsciously rubbing your face or brushing your hair.

Mannerisms, in and of themselves, are neither bad nor good. Many of the ones listed above constitute necessary and effective "in-body" or "in-frame" movement, and may be useful in developing a character or revealing a TV personality. Problems arise only when the performer is not aware of his or her mannerisms and uses them inappropriately or repetitively. When the performer is not in control, eyebrows "hopping" up and down constantly or a mechanical smile flickering on and off become irritating.

Mannerisms can be studied with the following exercises:

EXERCISE I

Ask a colleague whom you are with daily to help you inventory your mannerisms. Study the list you are given and try to become aware of the circumstances under which you do each movement. For example, a mechanical smile may be present only when you feel angry, rapid hand gestures when you are excited.

EXERCISE II

Set up a portable camera and deck with a thirty-minute tape, and eat dinner or have a conversation in view of the lens. You will soon forget about the camera and have an invaluable record of your daily mannerisms. Watch the playback with a colleague if possible.

The third component of the performer's image is movement. Movement quality can be classified with a number of useful adjectives— choppy, staccato, heavy, lumbering, light, flowing, spastic and so on. Movement speed also varies. The combination of movement speed and quality produces a very defined image—relaxed, efficient, determined, aggressive pliable, submissive.

Exercises such as the second one for the observation of mannerisms will help the performer become aware of movement patterns. The three exercises listed below, combined with the information from the previous studies, should give a sufficient picture of movement quality and speed.

EXERCISE I

Discover your totem animal. A trip to the zoo is often helpful, although not always necessary, in discovering the animal a performer most resembles. You may move most like a bear or most like a bird. Whether you look like any animal is irrelevant. If you will imitate the movement quality of a number of animals, you will soon find one or two patterns that seem similar to your own. The animal then serves as a model for studying yourself.

EXERCISE II

Inquire of another actor with whom you work closely what creature, animal, person or machine you most resemble. See if and how your patterns of locomotion are similar to what was named.

EXERCISE III

Study how you make contact with the ground. Flat feet tend to produce a lumbering, heavy walk. Many people spring off their toes and thus seem bouncy, young and light. Such a walk usually appears rapid, while the flat-footed walk seems slow. Often studying the way in which the feet contact the ground will explain why a performer has a particular image and will enable desirable change to begin. Watching yourself in mirrors such as those found in a ballet studio will enable you to see your walk.

With the information you have from these exercises, write a full description of your image, including both a dynamic and a static view. Below is an example description.

> Susan Henning is twenty-five to thirty years old. She has short, straight brown hair that curls slightly over her ears. Her face is round and soft with a high forehead and jutting chin. She appears intelligent and stubborn. Her smile is quick and friendly. She is an attractive woman but not necessarily beautiful. She is five feet, eight inches and stands erect. Her height is noticeable. Her shoulders are high and give an impression that she is tense. Her small waist and generally thin body are among her best features. Her choppy, somewhat stiff walk is her worst characteristic.

Once such a description has been written, the performer can make changes. It is important, as mentioned previously, not to attempt to force the body into the mold of contemporary fashion and lose unique qualities. Any changes should be carefully considered. Often changes are impossible. It is wise to remember that dancers and singers frequently develop unique styles from limitations. An honest and interesting image is the goal, and the first step is real self-awareness. In the next chapters, specific techniques for creating and changing the physical image, finding the appropriate image and developing a flexible image are discussed.

The information you have gained from the exercises in this chapter must serve as the basis for any character you create and for the personality you chose to reveal. Unless the "self" is the basis, your work will lack integrity. Particularly in TV, which, as previously noted, has a documentary quality, dishonest or mannered work is extremely noticeable.

11

THE VOCAL IMAGE:
Using the Voice on TV

When sound came to Hollywood in the late 1920s, many actors found themselves without jobs. Their voices contradicted their physical images; they sounded irritating on the primitive microphones. Two problems—the vocal image and the technique for working on microphone—must be dealt with by every film or video performer. Many media theorists suggest that the effect of TV is approximately 70 percent audio, and much commercial video work is straight voice-over, narration and interviewing. In Chapter 2, there is a detailed discussion of microphones; in Chapter 9, blocking for the microphone is discussed. This chapter will deal with the performer's technique and image in voice work.

THE VOCAL IMAGE

The voice will create at least 50 percent of a performer's image. It will reveal age, sex, mood, social class, regional origins, as well as such qualities as credibility, sensuality and aggressiveness. As with the physical image, the first step in developing the voice is to have a clear picture of your voice. Listening objectively is often more difficult than seeing objectively. It is necessary to hear the voice on professional equipment. What a performer hears when he or she speaks, even off microphone, is not what others hear. The vibrations within the head make it impossible for us ever to hear our voices accurately when we are speaking. Most people are surprised the first time they hear themselves on tape and will often respond, "I don't sound like that!"

It's true, you don't. As we mentioned in Chapter 2, TV sound is "mono" or one-eared compared to our live two-eared hearing, and our ears tense and relax in response to changes in volume that sound recording systems cannot tolerate. In TV work, the way a performer sounds on professional equipment *is* the performer's vocal image, because the equipment works that way.

The first step in obtaining an objective view of your own voice is to have a fifteen- to thirty-minute tape of yourself made on professional equipment. The tape should contain several kinds of speech—a conversation, a news report and a dramatic monologue. If it is impossible to obtain such a tape, you can gather some information by asking a friend to help you with the questions below. Even with a professional tape, you will get the best results if you have others listen to the tape and fill out the chart. Most small home recorders record the voice with such poor fidelity that they may be only marginally helpful.

VOCAL CHECKLIST

1. Pitch (high, low squeaky, uneven; etc.)
2. Nasality (nasal: most air through the nose, tight mouth) (denasal: little or no air through the nose, the way one sounds with a cold)
3. Resonance (full, flat, hollow)
4. Volume (soft, quiet, loud, varied, constant, etc.)
5. Quality (soft, thin, weak, strong, harsh, crisp)
6. Pace (speed) (fast, slow)
7. Rhythm (sing-song, staccato, fluid, etc.)
8. Emotional tone (aggressive, authoritarian, sexy, sensual, fearful, shy, sly, etc.)
9. Articulation (crisp, clear, mushy, particular sounds emphasized or missing)
10. Accent (regional, ethnic, social)
11. Effect (pleasant, soothing, strident, shrill, etc.)
12. Age-range (general impression within ten years)

After having completed this check list by listening to your tape and having gained impressions from others, write a description of your vocal image such as the one below:

John Smith has a husky, deep voice. He speaks loudly and has a staccato rhythmic pattern with the last word of sentences emphasized. His articulation is crisp. He seems aggressive and the vocal quality is generally strong. The voice is pleasant to listen to when the volume is controlled. One would guess that he is a midwestern businessman of about forty.

The description should then be compared with the description of the physical image. A mature voice may help to make a young physical image more flexible, a sexy voice make the body seem more appealing, an aggressive voice make a performer seem larger. Generally, however, the relationship between the vocal and physical image should be a logical one. Otherwise, the effect is comic. The large man with a squeaky voice, the young girl with a slow baritone often produce laughter.

VOCAL TECHNIQUE

The checklist above includes the primary variables of the voice. Severe problems with resonance, nasality or pitch are beyond the scope of this book. Sources for vocal exercises are included in the bibliography. The list above is designed to help a performer develop a profile of the voice. Some corrections can be made by audio personnel, and other problems may be aided by the exercises listed later in this chapter. Before beginning the exercises, it is important to understand what the sound recordist can and cannot do to help the performer's voice. The work of the recordist is more fully explained in Chapter 2. Generally a recordist can do the following:

1. Use of filter or an attenuator to moderate pitch. High frequency sounds can be cut off or bass sounds emphasized.
2. "Ride gain" to control volume level changes within reason.
3. Use a "pop" filter or wind screen to control mild breath explosions.
4. Choose the most appropriate microphone and polar response pattern for the performer and particular situation.

A recordist cannot control the other variables on the checklist. This means that a recordist can do nothing to make a performer's voice interesting and little to control clarity. The performer must assume most of the responsibility for the voice. Generally a director and sound recordist will expect that the performer can, within reason, maintain a pre-set volume level, clearly articulate words, control the pace (speed) with which he or she speaks and avoid excessive breath explosions or excessive sibilance on *s* sounds.

TV work both limits and increases the effect of a performer's voice. A resonant voice with great pitch variety and wide volume range is far less important in TV work than on the stage. The speaker systems in most sets are poor in comparision with film systems or with stage acoustics. Thus, the outstanding vocal quality of Lawrence Olivier, for example, is not particularly accessible to the TV viewer.

Second, a performer cannot create a kinetic response in the viewer with sound. A sudden scream or hysterical shriek on TV has no particular physical effect on the viewer once it is pressed into the volume and frequency range of the broadcast and receiver systems. In live theatre, however, spectators flinch or jump at a loud or sudden sound. They lean forward and become silent to hear a whisper. The most vivid illustration of this loss of kinetic response is that of a gunshot. A stage audience flinches: people cover their ears and react vocally. On TV, with present-day equipment, we hear the shot as little louder than a normal voice, and we certainly do not anticipate it physically.

On TV, in contrast to the stage or platform, a performer gains significant vocal gesture and detail. The subtle shadings of the voice are heard. On stage, where the spectator two hundred feet away must hear, the small vocal gesture, the click of the tongue, the sigh, the caught breath or the half-spoken word is not effective. In TV work, all these sounds are useful as well as a "mmm" or a "uh" that vocalizes a pause. Random or careless sounds must be screened out, as such small vocal gestures take on the same significance as words. In fact, such details are not only permitted and accessible on TV, but some sounds are nearly mandatory if the speech is to have a conversational quality. The performer must therefore develop the ability to use such gestures but also, as with physical mannerisms, be in control of them.

Special consideration must be given in TV work to projection, articulation, pace, tempo and rhythm of the voice. Projection (also discussed in Chapter 2) is rarely necessary in TV work. While a dynamic microphone will require a louder voice than a condenser microphone, a performer rarely needs to speak louder than called for in normal conversation. If the nearest camera operator can hear, so can the microphone.

The difficulty for most stage-trained actors is that, even when they reduce volume, the voice still has a projected and therefore "stagy" quality. It is necessary to be constantly aware of the people to whom you are speaking if this quality is to be avoided. First, you should avoid thinking of all the studio personnel as your audience (unless, of course, there is a studio audience). Think only of your partners as the immediate audience. Second, remember the viewing audience is one to three people, four to six feet away. With these thoughts in mind you should be able to adjust the volume quality appropriately.

For futher work, you will find it beneficial to rehearse in the studio or in a studiolike space whenever possible. Generally, the projected quality exists only in such spaces. We rarely project in a home environment. Becoming aware of your normal projection level at home or in a meeting room will also be of value. Notice this normal level, close your eyes while continuing to speak and visualize the studio space. The first few times you try this exercise, your volume level and projected quality will probably change.

A final problem with projection is that of consistency. Before taping begins, a voice level will be taken on each performer. As explained in Chapter 2, the level is set to keep the voice, if possible, peaking near 100 on the VU meter. While the recordist will "ride gain" to keep vocal level changes from distorting, many beginning performers have difficulty in maintaining a consistent level. They become louder as the production continues, they give the recordist a level lower than they use when shooting begins or they shout the first words into the microphone. These problems are the marks of amateur performers.

Consistency is necessary when two or more actors are using the same microphone. With quick dialogue or spontaneous conversations, drastic volume changes between performers can be difficult to handle. You should practice being aware of the volume level of others and matching your voice with theirs. Generally in daily conversation this matching does take place; thus, what is necessary for TV work is simply an increased awareness.

Articulation in TV work must always be extremely clear. No microphone, recorder, or speaker will produce your voice with complete fidelity. Home receivers, as noted, have particularly poor sound. Above all else, clear articulation is mandatory when, as is often the case, the viewer hears the performer but does not see him or her. Visual cues provide great amounts of information, and when the viewer is deprived of such cues, articulation problems become all the more noticeable. Many TV jobs are for voice-over work. Even in commercials, only hands or feet may be seen or only the product viewed, while in dramatic situations, the camera may be on the listener for a reaction shot and not on the speaker, who is out of the frame.

Articulation is controlled by the tongue, teeth, lips and jaw. Poor articulation is usually caused by a tight jaw or by failure to move the tongue and lips. If you have articulation problems (people frequently do not understand what you are saying), you should check the following:

1. Does the jaw hinge seem tight or immobile? Can you allow your mouth to drop open easily? Can you open the mouth wide and move the lower jaw from left to right? Can you open your mouth widely in a yawn?
2. Is the tongue mobile? Run your tongue around the inside of your mouth, both behind and in front of your teeth. Stretch your tongue out and try to touch your chin with the tip. Next, try to touch the end of your nose with the tip.

If you have difficulty with any of these activities, then they should be repeated as exercises until you can perform them easily. Also you should carefully do the work for face and jaw relaxation suggested in Chapter 18. Below are some additional exercises for articulation. None of these will correct severe difficulties, but they will help to alleviate minor problems.

Illustration 20

1. Yawn and then place the heel of the hand (*see illustration 20*) in the hollow of the face just below the cheekbone. Fit the hand into this area so that the edge nearest the thumb just touches the point at which your ear is attached to your face. Slide the hand, with considerable pressure, down the face, over the jaw, and off. The jaw should be pulled down opening the mouth. Let the mouth hang open for five seconds at least. (illustration 20)

2. Make faces—truly grotesque ones—to exercise the lips, jaw and facial muscles.

3. Blow air through the lips, allowing them to vibrate.

Articulation can also be used creatively. Genuine control over enunciation will allow the performer to manipulate language in an interesting fashion. Elongation of vowels or emphasis on particular syllables can often bring a vocal track alive. Deprived of resonance and volume, articulation techniques combined with variety in rhythm and pace are necessary if the voice is to be interesting. Good advice to the TV performer might be "taste your words" or "enjoy the way it feels to make words in your mouth." Many people rarely notice what it feels like to make a given sound.

Generally, in TV a fast rate (pace) of speech is effective so long as pauses are carefully taken. "Talk fast and move slowly" is advice performers often hear. A slow pace does not seem to hold attention well. The pause, in a fast delivery, creates variety and allows the viewer time to absorb information. Since one can vocalize a pause or use a verbal gesture within the pause, it can have its own language.

Rhythmic variety is mandatory. A sing-song quality soon becomes boring and numbing. In fact, any consistent rhythm, whether staccato or flowing, will feel burdensome to the viewer. Skill in the use of vocal rhythms can add the variety lost in volume and pitch. It is wise to spend some time practicing reading with a series of different rhythms. It is not necessary for the sake of exercise that the rhythms be appropriate to the work. The goal is simply to develop facility with rhythmic variation. You might begin by reading two sentences staccato, then one flowing, and one sing-song, then arbitrarily return to the staccato pattern.

Finally, unique personal vocal characteristics, such as regional accents, can be limiting if you cannot control them. However, they should not necessarily be abandoned completely. It is best to be able to speak with a variety of accents, but it is not necessary to have the traditional midwestern announcer's speech. Often a regional accent or unique vocal characteristic is not only acceptable but even desirable and saleable. The goal in all cases is an interesting voice with flexibility and control.

12

WORKING IMAGES:
Types in Commercial Formats

Typecasting is a reality in most professional performance work, but especially in commercial television, where performers are cast according to their physical and vocal types. Many traditionally trained stage performers are dismayed when they first seek work in commercials and find that agencies are interested only in their appearance.

However unfair this practice may seem, it is nevertheless a reality and it actually has some justification. Rarely in TV work, and almost never in work on commercials or spots, are there lengthy rehearsal periods to develop physical characterizations. Second, as mentioned before, much TV work gives the performer only ten to fifteen seconds to create a character or image. In a three-hour stage play, a performer can carefully construct a character and image whose development the audience can watch. On stage, an actor has less need to be an instantly recognizable type.

In addition, any major physical changes, such as padding for added weight or the use of age makeup, require considerably greater care and expense for the close-up work of TV. Most producers do not want to expend the time or money to make a thin actor fat when they can hire a fat actor. There are, of course, exceptions, but ordinarily they are only made when an actor's name commands a large audience.

Even well-known actors are, to some extent, circumscribed by typecasting. Comedians usually play comedy and heroes don't often play villains. Certain actresses play only "glamour" roles, while others play only "housewife" parts. Given the realities of typecasting, any performer should spend time carefully identifying his or her most natural type and the variations of that type.

IDENTIFYING YOUR TYPE

The exercises below are designed to help the performer discover his or her type. Before beginning to use them, however, you should be aware of common pitfalls in working with type. Many performers fall into a trap by focusing on what they believe their image "should be" and cannot accept what their real image is. Others try to "be like" a well-known performer and by doing so lose their own uniqueness. While it is true that certain images are more attractive than others, there is a demand for a wide variety of types in TV performing. The "housewife" is often in as great demand as the "model."

There are three ways to begin to discover type. First, a performer can see where he or she best fits on a list of standard types such as the sample one given below.

1. Young hero or heroine
2. Young wife/husband
3. Middle age family woman/man
4. Young careerist
5. Hardened business man/woman
6. Mother/father
7. Grandmother/grandfather
8. Advisor: priest, counselor, "Mary Worth"
9. Professional expert: doctor/lawyer
10. Working man/woman: waitress, clerk, secretary
11. Outdoors person
12. Athlete
13. Artist
14. Teacher/professor
15. Law enforcement figure
16. Mafia or underworld figure
17. Teenager: healthy/happy
18. Teenager in trouble
19. Senior citizen
20. Any strongly ethnic type
21. Society figure
22. Playboy/playgirl

Types can be added to this list, or combinations made of the types listed. Try to select the type or types that seem most to describe you. Ask a friend to place you on this list.

Second, make a list of well-known TV personalities and situation-comedy characters; see which ones you believe you are most like and least like. Check your choices with others and see if they agree or disagree.

Third, ask three professional acquaintances to assume that they are casting directors. Ask them to carefully consider what three roles currently on TV you might fill. Also ask them to tell you which three roles (within reason) you are least likely to fill. If possible, find out the reason for their choices.

After completing these three exercises, you should begin to be able to define patterns. For example, if your type was the mature professional male, if you most resemble Walter Cronkite and if you were cast by all your colleagues as Marcus Welby, you can clearly define a type for yourself. If there was a vast difference between the choices you made and those your colleagues made, then clearly your self-perception is not accurate.

EXPANDING YOUR TYPE

Once a type is clearly defined for you, then it is important to see what personal characteristics seem to be creating this image and to decide how these characteristics can be manipulated to create a wider variety of types. For example, a soft voice, an authoritative manner and gray hair may be the dominant characteristic in the performer who is cast as Marcus Welby. Such a performer may also be able to play the "friendly grocer" or the "local priest." He might be a good interviewer, or do well at voice-over work for documentaries. A clear definition of your personal type is rarely too limiting. Understanding the type and boundaries it creates will enable you to approach and audition for jobs realistically.

INDIVIDUALIZING YOUR TYPE

Once you have a genuine understanding of your type, you must find your own uniqueness. Within the limits of your type, you must discover what you possess that somehow makes you more interesting than twenty-five others of the same type. "Homogenized images" rarely sell.

While the idea of a "model" or an "athlete" may seem an appealing way to describe one's type, such classifications are actually bland. It is usually the contrasting, even seemingly contradictory, aspects of a performer that make him or her unique. For example, the woman who types herself as a "teacher" may be unique in that she also projects a bouncy, comic quality. The athlete with a strong physical body may be extremely soft spoken.

"SPELLING OUT" YOUR TYPE

With the above points in mind, take the information you have from the exercises in this chapter, combined with the information from Chapters 10 and 11, and prepare a short description of your type for a casting director. For example:

> Jackson is a tall, heavily built aggressive man of twenty to twenty-seven. He is most suited to roles that suggest physical activity or athletics. He might well play a professional athlete. He is unique, however, in that he can achieve a gentle vocal quality and affable manner in contrast to his physical appearance. His type range could well include such variations as the "police/counselor," the "priest/athlete/teacher" or the "high school coach." He most resembles such personalities as _____ and _____. He would be a good choice for a sportscaster or a host on a sports feature show.

A performer can, with work and training, increase the range of "types" he or she can play. While age, height, facial structure and body type are generally unchangeable, such things as weight, manner and vocal quality are not. It is generally worthwhile to experiment (on camera, if possible) with a wide range of standard types to see which ones you can achieve and how. For example, if you defined your type as the "young matron," experiment in front of the camera (or a mirror) until you find what changes are necessary to seem the "playgirl," the "college girl," the "frumpy housewife" or the "young doctor." Often little more is necessary than small changes in facial expression and body alignment. Chapter 13 explains techniques that can be used to help make small adjustments that will increase the range of work available to a performer.

13

CREATING A CHARACTER

Rosie the Plumber to Solness the Masterbuilder—the range of characters in dramatized material on broadcast television is enormous. There are, however, basic fundamentals in the performer's job that carry through all forms of dramatic material. The purpose of this chapter is to review the fundamentals of creating a character for performance, and to note the special requirements that the character created for television must meet. This chapter is not a substitute for a basic acting course, but the points covered here are useful to any performer at any level of experience dealing with a character for TV.

The basis of any acting is the actor's self, the feelings, experiences, ideas and particular human reality that is found in the performer's personality and body. Anything developed by the actor, any images and devices worked up for performance, are rooted in the personal identity of the actor. What is presented in this chapter is a series of concrete suggestions for doing this very personal work in a systematic way. These suggestions include perspectives and vocabulary from the Stanislavsky System as well as concepts from contemporary psychophysical approaches to acting.

The other starting point for the actor's work is the script. The text of the dialogue is the basic frame of reference for everything the actor develops. The givens of the script provide the basis for insights about the character, the action line of the piece and all other necessary information for beginning character work. Script work is discussed in this chapter and in Chapter 14.

Simplification of effect is necessary to create a performance that looks honest and natural on camera. There are two ways to simplify for the camera. The first, by far the easiest and most common, is to go for the cliché, the obvious, the predictable and expected way of doing things. Commercial broadcast TV is full of such acting: smirks, mugging, commonplace and overdone reactions.

The other method of simplying for the camera is to carefully develop and motivate a complete performance, detailed and finished in every way. Each gesture is tied to a clear objective and is spelled out in small particulars that make the performance truly human and believable. Once the characterization has been planned thoroughly, the actor then begins the process of trimming and simplifying for the camera. Of seven bits of business involved in picking up a coffee cup in character, the actor selects one or two, the ones that perfectly capture the nature of the character and his or her immediate intention in the script situation. What emerges is *simple, clear, vivid* and *honest*—much different from the flashy cliché that is rooted in nothing. Careful character work will not produce complicated, fussy or artificial performances; with attention to the realities of television, actors can produce simplified but effective performances.

The basic job of performing a character is to act out a life "career," a full line of action rooted in the script and extending beyond what the writer has indicated. The character's "career" is a dynamic series of actions, stretching over a period of time, involving other people and situations, adding up to a consistent life pattern. Archie Bunker, for example, made a career of being threatened; he is a "Little Man" whose career started before the events on a show and continues after each segment.

The "career" of a TV character has to be fully developed at all times, complete with peaks and valleys, group responses and solo work, expressive highs and lows. The TV performer must be prepared to jump into this career at any point, at any time. In the theatre, an actor can "work through" a part; in the studio, the actor must be ready to take up the character at whatever point in his/her career is necessary. Compared to the theatre, TV acting requires a much more controlled, and at the same time a much more flexible, approach to character.

Described below are four basic areas for character development, as adapted to the requirements of TV acting. Each area is approached as though the performer had unlimited time and resources to devote to creating the character. Since such a situation is a luxury for most actors, the chapter closes with a summary: how to prepare character quickly and efficiently with the minimum time and resources available.

THE PHYSICAL BODY

The most direct way to find and place a character is in the performer's body. The body is the source of energy and feeling in performance, as in daily life. Bodies map the history of the individual: tension patterns, withdrawals and avoidances, building defenses; locked-in hostilities are revealed to the trained observer by the alignment and placement of the body. Personalities have a strong physical base and a direct physical expression. The performer must know her/his own body well and be able to identify what kind of feeling the body naturally projects—tension, ease, vitality, rigidity and so on. This basic personality picture, which the actor sends to the everyday world, must then be manipulated and arranged to fit the physical image of the character. Working with the personal image information developed in Chapter 10, the actor joins character and personal image in physical body work.

Television acting requires a strict control over the smallest details of the physical "self" created by the performer. The camera focuses closely on how a hand holds a glass or a cigarette. Despite the low resolution of TV images, body cues carry a great deal of information about the people appearing on the screen. The natural limitations of the performer's body can be rearranged and used to advantage in creating body messages that present a character for the camera.

Weight and Grounding

The first physical element for the performer to work with is the placement of weight. A low center of gravity, for example, suggests solidity, firmness, a sense of strength. Placing the weight higher, however, changes the entire sense of the physical person to one of weakness, vacillation, nervousness, instability. An "off-center" weight placement gives a different picture again, especially keyed toward obsession, bias, neurotic or unusual responses. Whether the weight is forward or backward, putting the body on the toes or the heels, changes the image of activity/passivity, aggression/withdrawal, energy/laziness. The relation of body weight to the ground (*i.e.,* supportive, detached, in struggle) is an indication of the individual's attitudes about his or her own "grounding" in reality: secure, tentative, conflicted.

The performer may experiment very simply with weight placement and gravity center merely by standing still (preferably without shoes) in a cleared empty space and then mentally shifting the weight center from front to back, side to side, as noted above. Concentrate on the sense of self associated with each use of weight. Once the kinds of feelings involved are clear, the performer may go on to experiment with simple movements while using different weight placements: walking, sitting and standing, picking up a cup. Eventually a clearer picture of the character will begin to emerge as certain body feelings tie into the performer's initial sense of the character. At this point, the actor is working inside out to develop the feel of the character's physical personality.

Breathing

The physical reality of a character can be further extended with the use of breathing. Perhaps the most basic body rhythms are established with breathing. Fast or slow, deep or shallow, abdominal or chest, mouth or nose, regular or irregular, the process of breathing fixes energy level and rate of response in a way that significantly affects behavior. Breathing patterns are a useful tool in working with dialogue, as the performer begins to work through the lines. Breathing is particularly helpful in building responses to another character in close-up reaction shots, where the actor has to develop simple, clear responses to off-camera action or dialogue.

Tension

The physical personality of the character can also grow out of a study of key stress points in the body. The neck, for example, stiffens and locks under pressure, repressed anger or rigid control. Shoulders hold hostility and endurance under strong demands. The diaphragm and stomach often retain extreme anxiety and fear. Buttocks, hip joints and the jaw hinge are used to lock in strong feelings and strong expression of any sort. Even the feet are a significant measure of the physical personality; tensed or relaxed, they indicate the individual's "stance" toward reality. Strong feelings can be experienced by tensing and releasing these body parts, and such material can be incorporated directly into characterization and line readings. Flexibility and rigidity in each of these areas are all useful barometers of how easily feelings occur for the individual.

Centering

The use of energy centers may be the most efficient method of developing a physical personality for a character. Energy centers are simply an imaginary focusing device, through which the performer organizes his/her energy into associations around specific points in the body. By leading with the nose, for example, most actors quickly contact feelings of inquisitiveness, arrogance, contempt. No special movements or exaggerations are necessary, merely focusing and heightening awareness of the nose as the center of the personality. Strong responses come also from the chin (belligerance, risk-taking), the feet (indolence, directionlessness), the pelvis (sexuality, indirection), the back of the neck (tension, control) and so on. Organizing a character around such a point is a quick way to contact dominant feelings that can become the foundation for a physical personality.

The associations developed with energy centers are immediate and obvious, although not the same for everyone. Behind the cliché, however, lies a fundamental truth about behavior. Such character actors as Gale Gordon have created brilliant characterizations out of simple physical mannerisms: using a tucked-in chin and pursed mouth, Gordon's Mr. Wilson, in *Dennis the Menace,* and Osgood Conklin, the principal in *Our Miss Brooks,* were each memorable characters. Gordon created simple but vivid physical images that fit TV limitations well.

Particular characterization problems can also be solved by a physical approach. Age can be added or eliminated by a careful use of weight centering; the lower and more forward the center, the slower the rate and the greater the sense of age. The state of a character's health is similarly affected by weight center and by breathing placement and depth. Illness is usually accompanied by shallow breathing in the upper respiratory tract. A whole range of states and conditions affecting personality and character can be created with a manipulation of basic physical variables: breathing, weight centering, balance, alignment, energy centering. The actor should experiment with these variables freely, off-camera and alone, until the foundation of the physical character begins to emerge.

Business

Once the background material and basic script work (see below and Chapter 21) are complete, the performer can return to the physical body to fill in characterization with detail work on mannerisms. Most physical mannerisms make some sort of statement about unrevealed aspects of the character's history and background. Occupational mannerisms are simple enough to create, since they refer to an absent but *concrete* environment: pencils between the fingers, papers shuffled, the sense of a badge on the chest, a usually worn hard-hat and so on. Other mannerisms can be developed from a sense of the character's early background: an unconsciously clenched fist, food hoarded or gobbled at meals, hands fluttered protectively around a face, eyes constantly checking the room for unseen danger.

Consistency is not important to the physical personality. On the contrary, what is often most interesting about any characterization is the contrasts and the contractions in the way the person is presented. A hearty, booming voice set against nervous, shifting eyes, or hands figeting with hair against a straight back and rigid neck, such contrasts create depth, interest, resonance. Since television acting works best with a few well-chosen details, the performer must choose carefully in creating the physical personality with simple broad strokes. Mannerisms and body cues should balance each other to suggest conflict, contradiction and complexity *without* getting fussy and heavy-handed. Even the shortest walk-on is a full person who must be interesting to be noticed.

Detail

Costume and makeup complete the physical characterization for the actor. The basic TV design principles governing these areas are discussed in Chapter 19. Choices in these areas are often made by production personnel, and actors rarely have full initiative in finishing off their on-camera image. Where some choice is possible, however, costume and makeup should be chosen on the basis of how they make the actor *feel*. Certain fabrics will contribute sensations of lightness or age, confinement or sensuality, and so on. Eyelashes add sophistication, disguise, control. A built-up jaw line or a mole on the nose may be the entire basis for a quick but clear characterization. While the on-camera effect is crucial, the performer's choices here are also a way of helping to build a complete sense of the body, hence the reality, of the character.

DEVELOPING BACKGROUND AND BIOGRAPHY

Archie Bunker is more than a good performance by Carroll O'Connor; he is a complete *idea* about a man, a life, a situation with a full history. Over the years, Norman Lear's writers had gradually built up a biography for Bunker in order to fill in exposition for the incredible number of episodes churned out to keep the show on the air. The work of preparing a convincing background/biography is, however, really the actor's job. A well-crafted actor is always in possession of a full history of the character, especially any history that would affect current script situations. Since broadcast television is often taped out of sequence, the actor must be able to jump in at any point necessary, making *that* point the here-and-now present. Only with a full sense of history are these kinds of "reality jumps" going to be possible. Even the briefest walk-on needs a background, an identity with a minimal history. Stage actors have weeks and even months in long rehearsals with directors and other actors to develop backgrounds and biographies; TV actors may well be expected to produce results primarily from their *own* preparation.

The degree of background/biography preparation depends on the size of the role, whether the role is repeated in a continuing work and on the time available for preparation. Even for the smallest or simplest dramatic role, some information is needed: the actor should always know *why* the character has come to be here, what she/he wants here, and the reasons for her/his departure. A concrete background can well explain these reasons in biographical terms. A journal or working notebook is a good place to fix any information that the actor may wish to consult later.

Developing a character biography—a technique first associated with Stanislavsky System-trained actors—begins with the "givens" provided by the script. Any information in the diaglogue, especially in exposition, but also in the way other characters speak *to* and *about* the character, is crucial for background. The way the dramatic situation is described in the text adds other information. The director, production staff, and—when available—the writers themselves will often give further nuances and interpretations to the character. The actor's job is to take this often nebulous, impressionistic material about a character's "qualities" and project it into concrete data about a character's history, motivation and present objectives. Such material need not be shared with anyone, unless the actor senses that he/she is working on an interpretation that is inconsistent with that of the director or other actors. Background work is merely part of the actor's job, a necessary preparation for making something believable in front of the camera.

Presented below is a biography questionnaire that can be used to sketch out the background of a character under preparation. Selected parts or the entire form may be used; other questions may well be more pertinent to a particular character. The actor should reason backwards from the "givens" of the script, using fantasy and logic to construct a sort of dossier on the character. All background material projected should account for significant events, relationships (and such that affect the "present" of the script.

Contradictory elements are fine—they help keep the tension and conflict of the present in focus so that the *motion* of the character toward something is clear. Variety and contrast in background keeps the character flexible, with some range of possible responses in the *present*. Of course, as long as the character biography is consistent with the "givens" of the script, only the director or writers are judges of the accuracy of the invented history. The overall interpretation of the material has first priority; the actor's work must harmonize with it and extend it further.

CHARACTER BIOGRAPHY INVENTORY

Character Name _____ Nickname/Other Name _____
Age _____ Current Health and Physical Condition _____
Size _____ Attitudes about Body _____
Distinguishing Physical Characteristics _____
Date/Place/Circumstances of Birth _____
Parents' Names and Backgrounds _____
Attitudes toward Each Parent (past/present)_____
Siblings' Names; Attitudes toward Each _____
Family Ethnic, Socio-economic Status _____
Geographic and Religious Factors in Upbringing _____
Nature and Extent of Education; Attitudes about It _____
Significant Accidents and Illnesses _____

Occupation _____ How Chosen _____
Relations with Co-workers, Boss _____
Major Love Affairs and Relationships _____
Taste in Art, Music, Reading, Entertainment, Recreation _____
Favorate Activities: Childhood, Adolescence, Opening Adult, Present _____
Significant Experiences: Childhood, Adolescence, Opening Adult, Present _____
Things Character *Most* Wants Others to Know about Past _____
Things Character *Least* Wants Others to Know about Past _____

Once this material is developed, the actor must integrate it with body work to help make a concrete, realistic physical personality. Character biography puts the actor in control of the *logic* of the character. Within reasonable limits, the actor can tell what the character would or wouldn't do or say and so on; how she/he would react with others, speak, dress, eat. Again, considerable flexibility is necessary. The writers', director's or designers' requirements may be totally different from what the actor sees as reasonable for the character. An elaborate profile of a truck driver walk-on may produce a complex, interesting personality; if the director of a thirty-second spot needs a short and vivid entrance/exit, the actor's background work could be cumbersome or actually get in the way. Again, the overall interpretation of the material takes precedence over the individual actor's inclinations. The actor's job is to motivate, to make personal sense out of what has to be done. A character biography may be a useful tool in making the actor's work consistent, connected, personal and honest.

CAREER

Most people have a sense that they are on their way *from* something *to* something. Sometimes a person is not conscious of his/her journey, though everyone else can point out the pattern. At other times, a person will plan and control his "trip" down to the smallest detail—only fate or accident will knock him or her off course. People's lives are always in motion, whether conscious, unconscious, or accidental. The pattern of this motion, as well as the actual details, can be described as a *career*.

TV does not leave the actor time to develop an elaborate career. Tight focus and rapid cutting require, as noted before, a rigidly controlled image for the camera. Commercial work needs even further control. Thirty- and sixty-second mini-dramas require full characterizations that must be established instantly and that must change and grow in the service of the message. As with body work and background development, a character career must be planned out and immediately available to the actor at work. Rosie the Plumber should be fully there, on call, to deal with any kind of situation as her life goes on.

Planning Careers

In starting to work up a character career, the actor should begin with the question, "What do I (Rosie, for example) most want?" The answer to this question will be suggested by the dialogue, the writer's descriptions and other specifics related to the actual shooting script. The answer should lie somewhere between the immediate (*i.e.*, a raise, a spouse) and the cosmic (*i.e.*, love, security). Based on background work, the actor should refine the answer to arrive at something specialized for this particular and unique character. In traditional acting terminology, the answer to the question is the character's *objective*. Since performing is an active "doing" of a character, the objective is best expressed in terms of a verb—something the actor can try to *do* as the character. If Rosie the Plumber most wants to feel okay socially, the actor doing Rosie may phrase her objective as "I want to make everyone admire my competence (as a plumber)." This objective may work well for one episode for Rosie.

Changing Objectives

The objective is a good way to trace a character's career from scene to scene. Each scene will need a separate application of the objective to the specific circumstances of that scene. Episode 12 of Rosie might begin with a scene where, applying her objective, Rosie wants to impress Jane with her skills with a crescent wrench. By the fourth scene, Rosie's career may have evolved to the point that her immediate objective now is to avoid Bill and Charlie at a party (because they are better with a wrench than she has pretended to be). The changes in immediate objectives from scene to scene chart the direction of the career for this particular episode. If any particular scene objective seems unrelated or contradictory to the overall objective, either the overall objective is incomplete or inaccurate or the actor may not have understood the scene properly. Rosie should be Rosie, all the way through.

Change is often the key to the character's career. The actor should look at the script with the question, "How am I different at the end from at the beginning?" Once the points of difference are clear, the actor can question *why* the differences have developed. Objectives are met, frustrated, modified, abandoned. The actor must be clear about what choices the character makes in the face of change, and how these choices affect the general motion toward objectives.

Time Lines

Actors deal with careers in the present, in the here-and-now described by the script. The developmental line of the character has a past as well, and the actor must keep a consistent line from background biography through the permutations of the script, to an imagined, possible future that extends beyond the present episode—even if it is the only probable appearence of the character. Careers are lifetime affairs. Drama usally deals with heightened reality, the moments when a character's past/present/future all exsit together and change is imminent. Rosie's struggle with a balking sink sells scouring powder, but it also gives the TV audience a view of her struggles in her own life, with getting what she wants (however humble or banal).

Body and Career

The development of a character career must be carefully tied to the actor's body work for the character. Career changes require body changes. Success or failure with objectives will have marked effects on spinal alignment, shoulder placement, breathing. Physical mannerisms will change as well. The careful, craft-oriented actor choreographs these changes very specifically, scene-to-scene and line-to-line. In private rehearsal, the actor can try on a range of body behavior to match each point in the career. Extremes of behavior—especially in breathing, placement and movement rate for mannerisms—can be tried until the right combination seems natural. The "How am I different?" question asked above in career terms should also be answered in body terms, moment by moment. In private rehearsal, the actor can run through the character's entire career strictly physically, while running lines silently or listening to them over tape cassette. In studio rehearsal, this body work must then be adapted to blocking, camera work and choice of shots. Some of the most brilliant body gestures, planned to illustrate character career, may well not make it onto the final tape. The actor must stay flexible and rely on the director's eye to apply this material appropriately.

CHARACTER AND SELF

The raw material for the character is the actor. When you fantasize about the character's responses and background, you can only do it *with* and *from* your own experience. In fact, the close identification of character and self can be a very efficient way of working. Insights come quickly when the character is not too distant from what you already know. Energy is readily available when the responses feel natural to you and close to your own.

The person about whom it is most difficult to be objective is yourself. When you work in such a highly personal manner, the risk of sloppy, self-indulgent and self-deluded results is extremely high. An honest, well-crafted performance is a careful and difficult balance between an objective control of the performance product and a subjective investment of your own feelings and attitudes. Getting this balance is not always easy.

Comparisons

Some basic questions should be asked as you develop the character at various stages. The simplest, and maybe the most important, is "How am I different from/similar to _____ (the character)?" Traditional Stanislavsky Method acting asks the question as the "magic if": "If I were this person in this set of circumstances, how would *I* react?" Once you have the differences between your natural reactions (to other people, to events in the action) and the character's reaction in the script, you can begin to set out where you come together and where you don't.

Contrasts

Differences—such as a quick temper, easy defeat, shyness, indifference—are important. They shouldn't be dismissed or explained away lightly. Your own slowness to anger may make you uncomfortable with the character's temper, but you have to deal with it convincingly on camera, like it or not. Background and career work should help you understand such differences, and body work will allow you to root it in yourself physically.

For example, a nasty temper can be made playable in this way. Looking at the character's career may reveal a series of maddening frustrations in failing to meet objectives. A pattern of rebellion against authority figures might be placed in the biography. Anger can be bunched into high shoulders and clenched in a rigid neck. So the character can be a coiled spring, angry and itching to explode, for the big confrontation scene with the boss. The temper explosion becomes a natural and easy extension of the planning and preparation you have done. Instead of relying on flashy stage technique—nearly guaranteed to look ridiculous in TV scale—you can build and control the reactions you need, no matter how far from you they are.

Handling Differences

Characters far different from your own experience present a lot of problems, especially in TV acting, where stage tricks look absurd. Class and age differences are particularly difficult to deal with, because life experience is so unbridgeable. Success here depends on the actor's willingness to hang onto a clear sense of oneself on the one hand, while investing a great deal of energy in relating to the character's social reality on the other. You cannot *be* the character or truly know the character's experience; if you forget who *you* are in the acting process, you can only produce a sentimental imitation of your impressions of the character. The TV audience sees only what the cameras see, and the cameras merely record what's there. Honest acting for televison is rooted in this understanding.

Let's assume you are portraying an older waitress in a small diner for a single short appearance in a TV police show. You are an upper middle-class young college graduate with a few serious acting credits, all parts close to your age and background. Something about your type got you cast, and now you have to deal with a really distant character. Where to begin? First of all, with the differences. Mary, the character's name, is probably overworked and exhausted, according to the script (a problem you don't face yet!). She's exhausted because of all the demands made on her at work, all the people who want things from her.

As you think about it, you have an aunt/cousin/family friend who has lots of kids and who is similarly exhausted all the time. She doesn't seem to have a good picture of herself, so she gives in to any criticism and unreasonable request with a passive, depressed acquiescence. On the other hand, she has the money to get help if she wanted, so this useful personal parallel only goes so far. Mary the waitress is *really* trapped—by her age and experience, but most importantly by the social system that keeps her down. How do you act when you are trapped in a negative place by seemingly unalterable circumstances?

Taking your aunt's behavioral pattern and your own depressive reactions to limitations, you have the beginnings of an insight into Mary's character and situation. You then begin to look at how Mary copes with the situation, compared to the way you might. How does she resist (where you might see resistance as futile or childish)? How does she cooperate with the system of which she is a part (where you might sabotage it, retreat or opt for something else)? Looking at her waitress tasks, how would *you* do them in her situation? How would you get plates on and off the counter when it's just a job to be done efficiently? Taking your insight into Mary, you can build an effective portrayal of her by dealing with *her* adjustments to the situation. Where you are similar, the conclusion is easy. Where you are different, you must build a careful understanding of what she does that is different, why she does it that way and what her reasons are for doing things as she does.

DOING IT QUICKLY

You arrive at the studio at 7:00 a.m. to pick up a script. You are sent off to do location work and you memorize your lines on the way.

Makeup is done quickly, costumes are checked, you run the lines with the other actor. Then you are told that you have twenty minutes on your own before they need you for lighting adjustments and audio-level readings. That is the amount of time you have to prepare the character. With no time for elaborate preparation, how do you make a believable, honest, detailed character that you can stay with through twenty or more takes (all day!) under difficult working conditions?

Rarely will you have the time to do elaborate character development procedures suggested in the preceding sections. Sometimes it's not even worth it—developing an elaborate career for a walk-on may really be a waste of creative energy. Outlined below are steps that can be taken quickly to build a viable character under typical working conditions. If you have the need for more work and the time to do it, each step can be expanded, based on the previous discussion.

Working Conditions

Try to find a space alone if you can. Even a bathroom will do; if the weather permits, a walk around the block is useful. Take notes on the script, in the margins, on the back. While moving around, you can try all kinds of things: lines, gestures, stance, balance. Try simple tasks like opening doors, test your voice level, go over tricky words and typical enunciation problems.

Even if you are waiting just off-set, you can politely withdraw from the people around you and run things in your head while moving around the immediate area. You need not feel self-conscious; any working professional will respect your need to prepare your work. Stay with the script and avoid natural distractions. Nothing exists but the character and you right now.

Physical Body

Begin by experimenting with a posture or physical attitude that seems to express how your character faces the world. Make this into a stance you can move with and carry through your blocking, a stance that suggests *how* the character will meet whatever is coming his/her way. Then begin to extend the basic attitude by quickly choosing an energy center—a part of the body to focus on and work from. Add specific gestures and mannerisms that will punctuate the lines and the action. While some of these reinforce the attitude and center, some should contrast with them, giving complexity and variety. Check out breathing rate and balance and adjust them to attitude, center and detail work. The chart in Chapter 18 will help you complete the physical body preparation.

Applying It

Let's assume that you are doing a thirty-second public service spot on veterans' benefits. You are playing Bill Davis, a working-class vet, who is speaking from the lobby and counter area of a government office building about newly available benefits. The script is not too detailed about the character, but the director will give you feedback on what you create.

You begin with a certain belligerence you find in the lines, and place this feeling in your chest and shoulders. A low center of gravity and slightly flexed knees gives you a springy, athletic quality, while letting you work from the chest and shoulders. You try centering from the chin, which increases aggressiveness. Short, choppy gestures done near the face add masculinity, directness, and accommodate close-ups. Leading with one shoulder (assuming that lighting will allow it) opens the body and face into a quarter profile, creating a sense of self-protectiveness that goes with the lines. Chest breathing reinforces the body image and gives the voice a lower, deeper timbre. Weight is carried low, leaving a rooted planted impression. All of this preparation should take about three minutes to work out, allowing for trial and error. By now you have a defined body and a physical sense of who the character is.

Background

Where has the character recently come from and why is he/she there right now? What is the purpose of the entrance or first appearance? What is the strict, chronological sequence of the action in the script, both real and suggested? Where will the character go upon leaving the action?

A short biography can be generated in a few minutes, with notes taken onto the script. At least you can answer the basic questions of age, health, family status, social/economic/ethnic status, geographic area, work experience and so on. Double-check the givens in the script, and build outward from them. Take any "qualities" you are given (attractive, bitchy, disagreeable) by the writer or director, and turn them into specific data on the character.

Taking the vet spot example again, you have been told that Bill Davis is a white, working-class male in his late twenties who saw active duty in Vietnam straight out of high school. The tone of his dialogue is aggressive, and the theme of the veterans' benefits material suggests self-improvement, possibly ambition.

With these givens—easily available from the script and from the director—you can fantasize a consistent background quickly. Let him come from an industrial Northern city—say Detroit or Cleveland—with a staunch blue-collar tradition. Given him an inner-city upbringing, with a strong will to survive and the necessary combativeness to cope. He has a good manual job (possibly construction), but he is subject to lay-offs and has little economic security. Yet he has been through a great deal in Vietnam, and feels entitled to more than he is presently getting. He is upwardly mobile: aggressive, ambitious, slightly suspicious of the obstacles that always seem to crop up. He wants a better job, with more prestige and security, and needs the training to get one. Veterans' benefits may hold the key.

Once the background and biography have been projected, you can deal with the immediate circumstances of the script. Most of the dialogue is directly addressed to the camera—to veterans, their family and friends—except for a final scene where Bill Davis completes an application in the office with a clerk. You might decide that it is a Monday morning, on a day taken off from work for the purpose of applying for the new training benefits. Therefore it is costing Davis something, and he is taking a risk for a possible future. He is in work clothes, and possibly has just gotten off the bus or parked his car (older, needs expensive work).

He has no formal exit from the scene; there is just a dissolve. However, you might see him stopping for a beer after this trip to the office, perhaps with his work friends at lunch. This image suggests a way to handle the direct camera address—you might see him talking informally to friends about the vets' benefits as something he is entitled to. Bill, like his buddies, wants a bigger "piece of the pie." They talk about it a lot, with a class-related resentment of what their present share is.

By this time, with only a few minutes' fantasy and projection, you have assembled a potent biography and a working background for the scenes to be shot. Bill Davis should now tap a reality for you that can be used throughout the shooting.

Career

What does the character want right now? How is he different at the end than at the beginning? What changes and why? Charting a progress toward the character's objective, you will build a physical and psychological career in detail.

We have already projected the overriding concern for Bill Davis: getting ahead and getting more. His immediate career starts as he makes his entrance into the office in the first scene. He has come there to get the means to get what he wants. He then tells the camera/viewers what he is entitled to and why, justifying his action with the tone and phrasing he uses with his buddies. Filling out the application with the clerk, he meets no resistance as he goes ahead toward the objective. In the final address to the audience, he can express satisfaction and success at the probability of completing this phase in his (and, by correlation, their) career.

His objective can be stated in a verb: to get what he is entitled to. The impact of the objective affects his attitude toward the other characters in the piece—the clerk, with whom he is assertive, and the camera/viewer, whom he includes as acquaintances familiar with his problems and aspirations. He begins aggressively, but relaxes (physically and vocally) as no resistance is met on the way toward his objective.

Character/Self

You are not Bill Davis, but you have dealt with enough faceless bureaucracies to understand his stance toward the world. Focusing on the differences between you, it may be necessary to deal with class and work attitudes to make the characterization convincing. If you are college-educated and articulate, you may not be as intimidated by government agencies and the hurdles they present. You may deal with frustration more artfully, and your body may not be your primary means of expression and action (as Davis' body is to him).

Nonetheless, his situation is accessible to you. You now have the tools to make him come to life on-camera. The character will grow for you as you have more chances to think about specific lines and phrases. Trying things with other performers—experimenting with various rhythms and tempos while responding to their own character development—will add considerable depth and richness to your work (see Chapter 16). Above all, you must stay responsive to the input of others in the working situation. Although you have developed something dynamic with which you can create an honest, believable character, you *never* perform alone. The reality that exists in the camera and on the screen is dependent on the work of many others. Take what they are doing, thinking and planning, and use it as part of your own performance.

SUMMARY

The material presented in this chapter is a summary of a system useful in preparing a TV performance. It is, however, *preparation*. The actual process of acting on camera involves some special considerations that are a very real part of the television medium. In the next chapter, we will examine the process of developing the role in production on TV.

DEVELOPING THE ROLE

14

The actual reality of performing on-camera is the culmination of the character preparation discussed in the last chapter. But there is an important difference between the preparation and the doing. The actor analyzing and evolving a character is taking an abstract idea and elaborating it. The actor performing a part is really doing something concrete. *Character* is who you are: *role* is what you do. Finally, it is the role that the actor develops on the camera, for the audience; character is really an abstraction which is useful to the script writer and to the actor in preparing the performance.

Most people play a variety of social roles: student, employee, lover, parent, revolutionary. These roles are defined by the context they are performed in and by the purpose of the person performing them (*i.e.,* make money, care for a child). The dramatic role delineated in a script can be approached in a similar way. The purpose of this chapter is to put TV performance in the context of *action* and of *time*. The performer needs a few basic tools to convert character into role, to make the part live through the time of the performance. An actor who *only* portrays a fixed image of a character is static, unresponsive. A really effective performance is alive and appears spontaneous; the actor truly listens and reacts in the here and now. Outlined below are several basic traditional devices for developing the role, which are adapted for the reality of TV acting.

SCRIPT WORK

Not only does the dialogue of the script give you the profile of a person to perform (character), but the lines also trace this person through a series of events to some kind of conclusion to her/his situation. During the time you spend with the script prior to performing, you must carefully focus on the *action* suggested in the writing. How are things different at the end than at the beginning of the scene, of the whole piece? What is the story, outlined in a few sentences? What precisely is your part in the story? How do your character's objectives mesh with this action? Deal with verbs as much as possible to pinpoint the action and your role within it; as before, avoid adverbs and adjectives that just describe static qualities.

Script work also involves digging beneath the surface of the dialogue to find the meanings that are hidden in each character's phrasing and style of expression. The truth (of feelings, beliefs, intentions) is rarely on the surface. How to actually speak the dialogue is not your first concern—that will emerge as meaning becomes clear.

Actors often get trapped in wording and phrasing, which can deflect them from the personal reality of the part. One of the best rehearsal devices to free yourself from the words is paraphrasing. Go through the text line by line and put the dialogue in your own words, in your own habitual manner of speaking. Phrases that stop you are not clear enough to you; if you attempt to perform them as is, you will be wooden, flat, without depth or texture. If other techniques fail, ask the writers or the director to paraphrase tricky sections for you so that at least you will have their intentions and interpretations clear. Paraphrasing often reveals an awkward or inappropriate word choice in scripts, which can sometimes be rewritten. Paraphrasing works best with other actors to cue you *before* you memorize the actual wording of the script. Memorization without paraphrasing tends to fix inflection and rhythm, before you are certain that your reading is appropriate. In performance, however, the text is sacred; the performer has a professional obligation to speak every word as written. Ask the director's permission before you change or omit *anything* in the script.

SUBTEXT

Another valuable technique for opening up the script for yourself is the development of a subtext. Briefly, subtext is the meaning underneath the dialogue, the words under the words. A simple phrase like "May I have a match, please?" can mean a variety of things, from "Please pay attention to me for a change," to "I'd really like to sleep with you." A major part of the performer's job is to fix on the subtext and to illuminate it in a performance. Stanislavsky is reputed to have said that people come to the theatre to hear the subtext of a play from the actors; if the audience were only interested in the text, they would have stayed home and read the script. The simultaneous presence of text and subtext is what makes a performance live, what gives it tension and depth.

Subtext is different from paraphrasing, which is merely finding another way of putting the dialogue to underscore its surface meaning. In developing subtext, you must decide what the character really means in each line, what the intentions and objectives are in each phrase and word. Sometimes text and subtext coincide, and the character means/intends exactly what is said. When both levels diverge, however, the performer must decide concretely on what the character literally has in mind.

Subtext should be written down in the script in the early stages of script work before the lines are memorized. In rehearsal, directors will occasionally call for the actor to speak the subtext or to physicalize it in a gesture, a posture, a way of handling a prop. Making the subtext concrete in this way enriches the performance enormously; the actor can do such work alone if no other opportunity emerges. In performance, the director and the actor decide together how much of the subtext is presented directly and how much is hinted at with inflection, pauses, timing, gesture. The recipient of the meaning of the subtext is rarely the other characters; it's usually the audience itself. The camera—which can help to underscore subtext by cutting, point-of-view and reaction shots—serves as the viewer's eye in watching the character reveal the truth beneath the surface.

LEARNING LINES

Once the role has been developed through script work, paraphrase, and subtext, you can begin to memorize the dialogue. If possible, you should spend some time with other performers on line read-throughs. Your sense of rhythm, timing and inflection has been set in your own preparation, and you can now adjust to the delivery of those you are working with. Repeated runnings of dialogue *together* makes memorization much easier. If you do this work alone, make sure you run the lines aloud, covering your own with an index card. Learn at least a full sentence of cue line so that you have no confusion on lead-in and so that you have plenty of time to control your response. Your cue pickup should be so flawless that you can concentrate completely on your immediate response in the scene. Fumbling for a cue destroys concentration and flow.

MOMENT-TO-MOMENT PLAYING

Your total involvement in both the character and action must be coupled with a tight focus on the "present" in the scene. The here-and-now reality of the situation can only be created by the performer's complete commitment to the action, to moving through it point by point. A major indication of your skills in moment-to-moment playing is your ability to *listen*. If you in any way appear to expect what you hear, the illusion of the present is destroyed. Focus on each word spoken to you and absorb its impact. Concentrate on your objective and evaluate what you listen to in terms of it. Expect nothing, and allow your responses to flow through you. Ask your director or anyone coaching you to watch carefully for any instances of *anticipation,* any point at which you *telegraph* what is coming next. Moments of blankness and inertia are a sign that the scene has lost its reality to you, that you are no longer in the present. Your role is composed of a pattern of action that your character follows and responds to, and you can only be at one point on this pattern at a time.

One rehearsal technique for helping moment-to-moment playing is a game of catch. You and a scene player can begin to toss anything back and forth—a shoe, a milk carton. As you get comfortable with the game, begin the dialogue. Don't make anything happen with the game; simply let yourself respond to the situation. Catch can turn into keep-away or even tag, depending on the action and the subtext. The game interaction forces you to stay in the present, and the action opens up the dialogue in a fresh and spontaneous way.

INNER MONOLOGUE

Your conscious mind is never completely at rest. Stray thoughts, phrases and images float through constantly, or spiral away toward the periphery of whatever you are concentrating on. A crucial technique for performing a role is the development of an inner monologue, a constant flow of thoughts and ideas that come from the core of the character you have developed as she or he responds to the present reality of the scene. The inner monologue is an extremely useful tool for using subtext to create moment-to-moment playing. An inner monologue is an actual stream-of-consciousness verbalization of everything going on in the character's head. You put into words your character's conscious thoughts, unspoken subtext, half-conscious dreams and associations. In rehearsal and preparation stages, it is often useful to actually verbalize your inner monologue. By letting this material flow freely out loud, you can soon pinpoint those places where you aren't really clear what your reaction is, or what your real motivation is in making a choice.

Creating an inner monologue is a process of free-association based on all the preparation you have done up to this point: background work, physical-body work, career and objective analysis, script and subtext and so on. Your mind and imagination can roam freely, using this material as touchstones. The inner monologue also keeps you in the present. You must respond to all the action in the scene, including your own blocking and gestures. You must focus completely on the present moment, watching and listening carefully to everything in the scene around you.

TV acting especially calls for the inner monologue—without it, the close-up and the reaction shot reveal the black emptiness of an actor who is somewhere else besides the scene. A random sampling of commercial broadcast TV will reveal instances of unfocused performing with no inner reality. Notice, for example, the announcer who misses his cue and is caught blank-faced on a live camera.

In short, using the inner monologue technique will help you to concentrate completely on the action as it is *presently* happening. It also keeps you aware of the *inner* reality of the character, which changes from moment to moment. By verbalizing all available feelings and thoughts, you directly experience the role in action in the scene.

PLAYING OBJECTIVES

The stage actor works with a continuous performance; in most conventionally written plays, he or she has a linear career to act out through a linked series of immediate objectives. Playing objectives is a more complicated procedure in video acting. The biggest problem is the discontinuity of performance. While some big-budget network shows are shot straight through with all cameras rolling and edited later (*e.g., All in the Family*), some variation of film-style shooting is much more common. Since film-style shooting is done a few shots at a time, the performer usually works in small, odd fragments of time (see Chapter 17). An organic analysis of a script into natural segments of action can be a waste of time, since the actor probably won't get to work this way anyway.

If you have done the preparation suggested in the previous chapter, you will be clear on the kind of career the character has, as well as the objective she or he is pursuing. This objective still has to be broken down into a series of immediate objectives that link each action together to shape the role. The actor flows from one to the next in the inner monologue, and notes the change points in moment-to-moment playing. As one objective is met (*e.g.,* to ask for a match), the next begins (*e.g.,* to ask for a date).

Little of this internal work may show in the shooting and cutting done to prepare a tape. Such acting is especially difficult under the conditions prevalent in most studio and location work. The natural phrasing of the scene, at least from the actor's perspective, may be completely disrupted by the blocking and shooting necessary to record it properly.

You should begin with a shooting script, or with a clear understanding of how the material will be cut and arranged for shooting. The units of time to work from are those created by the cutting and switching of the camera. Each single shot you are on camera is a link in the action. Plan a limited, concrete objective for each shot. Be particularly clear on reaction shots, since you will not have dialogue to carry you. The series of limited objectives you have must add up to a vivid statement of who you are as a character, what you have experienced and done in this segment of your career.

Precise camera blocking and the absolute necessity of meeting your marks on set make it mandatory that you focus your objective within a small bit of action. "To light her cigarette" is still too broad an objective when the shot includes only her cheek in profile and your right hand with a match. Instead, make it "to control the movement of her head with my match." They you have a single gesture in a single shot to complete the objective. A generalized objective leads to broader, less refined performing. The results are sloppy technically and much less clear in terms of characterization.

Entrances and exits are part of the natural timing of the stage performer, but the TV camera often eliminates them. Without such specific beginnings and endings, you must use carefuly defined objectives to mark off the rhythm and phrasing of the role. Begin the take with a clear sense of intention that will control the force of an opening gesture and the sharpness of inflection in your first spoken word. Clear conclusions must be sought in a similar way. The final shot of you in any given series should carefully resolve your last immediate objective: either you get it or you don't, and you respond to that success or failure. Power is yours, or you get the girl, her money or whatever. Finish the last image with a sharp statement of exactly where you are at the end.

On the other hand, the TV actor often has to begin shooting in the middle of an action unit, possibly even at a peak moment of climax or just at a quiet resolution and fade away. Sharpness and force may be inappropriate. Takes are rarely planned around the natural builds of action for the actor. Whenever you start and wherever you finish a take, you must be clear on the *exact* point in the action for starting and stopping the take. Focus on the specific level of build or resolution and hit it precisely as you come in and out of the take.

Objectives that are developed and played according to the structure of the actual shooting will carry much more forcefully than those that are generalized from the dialogue. With this kind of clarity in your performance, your preparation in the role will survive (and probably even grow) through the tedium of repeated retakes. If you cannot get a shooting script in advance, develop your objectives as logically as possible, and then request a rundown on the shots in rehearsal. Find out what camera you are playing to and when, then adapt your preparation on the spot.

SUMMARY

Performing a role is a much different process from preparing a character. Action is the heart of the role. Developing the action involves setting the line readings, establishing the reality underneath the dialogue, working off other performers to fix rhythm and tempo and fitting the entire performance into the time and space structure made by the camera and the director. In this discussion we have suggested a number of ways to keep the performance fresh, spontaneous and fully in the present. Your performance will be further affected by the nature of the material you are working with. Chapter 16 will discuss the realities of genre acting and the special requirements of major types of performance.

15
REVEALING THE PERSONALITY:
Working without a Character

Unlike stage work, television often does not require the performer to develop a separate character or a role. As an information and entertainment medium, many TV formats require "personalities" rather than actors. A personality performer may be a talk show host, a newscaster, a narrator, a lecturer, an entertainer such as Dinah Shore or a sit-com star such as Marlo Thomas. An actor is a performer who creates a variety of characters, all somewhat different from the self. Personality performers, on the other hand, give the impression that they are the same on and off camera, that they are not creating characters but are presenting the true self.

While the difference between a "character" and a "personality" is quite clear at the extreme ends of the spectrum—Johnny Carson as compared to Maude—it is far less clear with Lucille Ball, for example. All well-known "personalities," however, share certain characteristics. First, they have established a particular relationship to the audience. Walter Cronkite seems like a parental advisor, Johnny Carson the mischievous friend, Lucy the scatterbrain next door.

This fixed relationship leads to a set of expectations on the part of the audience. Cronkite will be serious and Carson playful. We might well be shocked and offended to discover Carson giving a serious address on politics or Cronkite telling after-dinner jokes on or off the screen. Part of the appeal comes from the fact that we can trust these performers to behave according to pattern. Yet obviously Cronkite is not always serious nor Carson always humorous, and Lucille Ball is an intelligent, capable woman.

The personality performer's consistent image and "predictable" behavior on camera allows the viewer to identify with, and relate to, the personality in some specific way. We usually agree with Cronkite; we may admire him and seek to be as intelligent as he appears to be. We play with Carson; we let him be mischievous *for* us; we envy his boldness and wit. We laugh at Lucy; we feel superior to her. Viewers would expect to interact with these people in this same way should they meet them off-camera. While such a reaction from viewers might often be inconvenient for these well-known personalities, the corporate president might find it quite desirable. If, for example, he were perceived as a caring father in a video tape on company benefits, he might well find employees behaving with less hostility toward him.

We may feel we know TV personalities well—better than we know close friends. However, we know only the parts of them they have chosen to reveal. The skills they use in this process are not difficult to acquire. We all reveal different aspects of ourselves at different times. We each have our public self, our office self, our parental self and such. The skilled performer can control which self is revealed, when and how much. He or she can create a consistent recognizable image that, however limited, has the desired effect.

REVEALING, NOT BEING

In developing a performance personality, the key word is *reveal* rather than create. Successful public personalities are always grounded in some aspect of the real person. The problem in choosing which aspects of the self to reveal, and then finding the physical image and the behaviors that best display these traits. The most effective media personalities are developed through full self-realization. After all, the performance biography, career and body (described in Chapter 13) of the personality performer are his or her own, not those of a character.

Personality images that are far different from the self are usually either bland, artificial or embarassingly dishonest. Beginning performers and those people who perform only occasionally might be interesting and entertaining off camera, but lifeless or ludicrous on camera. They desperately try to avoid making mistakes, to appear controlled, to seem dignified, sexy or interesting The more they try to *be* rather than to *reveal*, the less successful they are. The young model who has just learned to "bat" her eyelashes or the aggressive salesman who has developed a "deep voice" make us uncomfortable, resistant to their appeal.

WORKING WITH GIVENS

In choosing what personality image to reveal for a certain performance, a performer must consider both *who he is* and *what he must do* (his function) in the show or tape. Certain physical characteristics are unchangeable and must be revealed. If a performer is clearly a member of an ethnic group, has a noticeable laugh or a round physique, it is best to accept the traits and manipulate them to advantage. In all probability they cannot be concealed. A prominent stomach is a typical example: allowed to show, it may be amusing or even given an air of solidness to a performer's image, while a half-concealed potbelly may look ridiculous. Jackie Gleason built innumerable comic bits off his body profile, as did Jerry Lewis off his height.

FUNCTION AND ROLE

Before deciding how to present the unchangeable aspects of physical self, before choosing what personal traits to emphasize, a performer must consider his reason for making a particular type or appearing on a particular show. While personality performers do not perform dramatic roles as discussed in Chapter 12, they have a particular function to fulfill for the viewer. This function operates in many ways like the role of the dramatic actor.

The combination of function and image is the basis of the personality presented by the performer. Both aspects of personality performing must obviously be compatible. The image is static, the function active, and both are interdependent. Lucille Ball's function is to entertain us, as is Johnny Carson's. Both Lucy and Johnny enter into an agreement with us; they agree to make us laugh. Walter Cronkite or Eric Sevareid also agree to entertain us, but their role includes an unspoken agreement to reassure us and make us feel in touch with our world. Barbara Walters' role in an interview may be to help us open up the guest, perhaps discover information the guest did not wish to share. To a certain extent she is the detective, Cronkite the teacher, Carson the clown.

Personality performers, like dramatic actors, also have a kind of subtext to their role. For example, Cronkite's message is not only the news (the text) but a subtext that says "I am trustworthy." His objective, to entertain us and reassure us, is accomplished through this subtext. Likewise a corporate president may present a text about the successes of the past year and the growth of the company. He may not only be saying "We have had a good year" but also "I am a good leader." His objective is to secure his position as president. Certainly talk show hosts usually have a subtext something like "I am entertaining, clever and amusing."

PHYSICAL PRESENTATION

These performers carefully mesh the physical characteristics they reveal and the gestures they use with the roles they fulfill. Many of the aspects of the physical body described in Chapter 13 are apparent here. Cronkite's physical stance toward the audience is direct and frontal, hands solidly on the desk, weight firmly rooted in the chair. His body seems as solid as his information. His movements are controlled and deliberate. Walters also uses deliberate movements and a direct approach, often in contrast to her somewhat nervous guest. Carson, on the other hand, stretches in a relaxed manner in his chair, is rarely frontal, and uses quick, frequent movement. Carson chooses to emphasize his hands and facial expressions, while Cronkite leads with his eyes; his head, the symbol of his intelligence, is the nearest part of his body to the camera lens. Julia Child teaches us to cook as much by her encouraging yet firm tone of voice as by her detailed instructions. Her direct eye contact with the lens and her gestures to camera include us so completely that we expect her to correct our every move. Her role is to teach, ours to learn. It is a role as clearly defined as the role of any actor playing a character.

OBJECTIVES

Even as guests on a talk show, the performers must clearly mesh their role and image to reveal the aspects of the personality they want to present. Most talk show guests are there to sell something—themselves, a new book, a new play, a new movie, a cause, a candidate, a piece of legislation. The talk show guest needs to pursue clear objectives if this task is to be accomplished. The guest may be the acknowledged expert who has been invited to discuss a public concern, or a well-known entertainer who has finished an autobiography. In either case, the producers believe this guest will be entertaining. The guest must decide exactly how he or she can best do so and fulfill his or her own personal objective. The expert may really want the viewer to take some political action, the entertainer, to sell his book. In another case, a new personality appears on a talk show for public exposure, to be seen as an interesting, beautiful, lively or funny new talent.

Obviously in the latter two cases, the objective is to present the personality itself as the product. Personality more than information will also "sell the product" in the earlier examples. The expert must reveal those aspects of his or her personality that emphasize intelligence and judgment. He or she may have a wonderful comic sense but that need be revealed *only* if it heightens credibility.

FIXING THE IMAGE

A consistent personality image has advantages and disadvantages for the performer. In the case of a corporate president or a new entertainer, a consistent image (with sufficient variation to create interest) is desirable. Media personalities like Cronkite, Carson and Walters have worked hard to be remembered and recognized through a consistent image. For actors, such consistent personality images may occasionally be limiting. For example, in the case of Lucille Ball, a particular image has been so imprinted on the public consciousness that it might be nearly impossible for her to play a serious role.

Career goals and needs will determine just how consistent or limited a performer's public personality should be. However, the skilled performer should certainly have the ability to be consistent.

REVEALING THE PERSONALITY IMAGE

Some simple techniques can help the performer begin to discover and reveal his or her public personality.

1. Identify any unchangeable or extremely noticeable traits (*e.g.*, ethnic identity, size and so on).

2. Identify the "personality" traits you most often reveal. Ask several acquaintances what they would say if given only three words to describe your personality. If, for example, the responses cluster around such traits as jolly, affable and playful, as opposed to intelligent, serious and aggressive, then a clear personality picture begins to emerge. Next, ask these same acquaintances what physical, vocal or behavioral traits lead them to describe you in this way. They may, for example, link the traits to a large stomach and a quick smile, or to rapid body movements and a frequent giggle.

3. Define the role you want to fulfill as clearly and concisely as possible. Define your objectives. Do you want to be the expert, the friendly advisor or the clown. Do you want to convince your viewers to do something, to like you or to laugh.

4. Select the traits that you most believe will reveal the image you want. Use not only the information from steps 1 and 2 above, but also the information from the work in Chapters 10, 11 and 12. Do not try to use traits you don't have.

5. Practice extending the traits you most want to reveal. Explore and extend the trait in an exaggerated manner in order to see all the possible ways of revealing it. You would in all probability not use the full extension in an actual show or tape. In developing a trait through extension, an exaggerated projection is most useful. For example, if you

wish to heighten your natural jolliness, extend the image all the way into Santa Claus; try out related gestures, smiles and laughter on a large scale. See how such an exaggeration affects your posture, breathing and vocal quality. If you wish to be seen as serious and academic, play an extension of yourself as the stodgy professor. How do you walk with this extension? How do you use your hands? You might also free-associate to the animal or creature that most nearly displays the trait you wish to reveal; explore the traits of this creature. Do you want to reveal the wide-eyed, serious side of yourself? Work with an image of yourself as a kitten or chipmunk. If elegance and beauty are your intended traits, a peacock may help. Learning to play with your image is very liberating, and will help reduce your ego involvement in the process of self-revelation.

6. Remember that simplicity is the key to effective TV performance. Select only a few traits to emphasize, and let other personal mannerisms complement them. A clear, accessible image must be presented; too many traits become confusing. Many noted personalities have developed their entire image off one trait, which has since become their trademark—Goldie Hawn's peculiar voice, Phyllis Diller's frumpyness.

7. Discover two or three particular gestures that best display the traits you want to reveal. For example, you may choose to emphasize your jolliness by your laugh, your rapid speech and your bouncy walk. Other gestures will also complement this image, but you should have at least three effective ones readily available. They should, of course be gestures that are natural to you, not created ones.

8. Be willing to let the viewer see your flaws, your peculiarities, your individuality. Do not try to hide behind an image you wish you were or believe you should be.

SUMMARY

Personality performance is a staple of broadcast television. Specific formats have their own individual requirements, however. In the next chapter we will survey the major styles of TV performance as they affect the work of the performer.

16

STYLES OF TV PERFORMANCE:
Genre Acting

Commercial broadcast television has a number of clearly defined genres—types of programs that reappear season after season with minimum cosmetic changes. Each genre has its own conventions that define its general content and style of production. The evening news and a police action show may occasionally look alike, but basically they are very different genres. Each new season brings in programs that overlap or recombine genres to give you standup comic cops or talk show parodies. These are anomalies, temporary novelties, usually replaced mid-season with a daffy sit-com or an inner-city shoot-'em-up. Commercial television seeks successful formulas to pull maximum viewing and high advertising revenues. Accordingly, it works with fixed defined commodities in its programming.

Even non-commercial broadcast TV and small-format video production is affected by genre programming, although artistic personnel in these areas are less likely to be bound by the strict conventions of commercial TV. PBS interviews may be more inventive or candid than network inteviews, but the general type of program is still the same. Even when video personnel work completely free of commercial considerations, they are preparing material for viewers who regularly watch commercial TV. Experience and expectation create a stylistic context for most TV production. As an actor you will work within this context. It is necessary to understand, and to be able to work with, the major styles of TV production.

Genre TV programming leads to genre TV acting. Each general style has its own set or requirements and specialized effects. Some are controlled by the actor, some by the actor's performance. To really understand the intricate details of television style, you have to watch a great deal of TV—a treasure trove of acting techniques developed early in the industry's life can be found in *Lucy* reruns and the ever-popular *Perry Mason*. It is possible, however, to make concrete suggestions about acting within the limitations of each major performance style. Summarized below are a series of observations for genre acting for each TV style, followed by a consideration of the major issues involved all TV acting styles.

SOAP OPERA AND DRAMA

The single-program drama and serialized ("continuing") drama are closest to the form of the traditional drama written for the theatre. Like the plays of psychological realism from which they emerged (*e.g.*, those of Arthur Miller, Tennessee Williams, Paddy Chayevsky), these scripts focus on character. Plots are manipulated arbitrarily to show people as victims (and victimizers). The action line of most continuing drama reduces to a simple formula of 3 R's: revelation, realization, reaction. The last term is especially important—soap characters are reactive. They are in constant turmoil from circumstances apparently beyond their control. These responses are the heart of the matter for the viewer. Illogicality of plot and arbitrariness of action is not important. The degree and depth of feeling provides both the content and the *form* of the soap.

Technically, the close-up shot is the stock-in-trade of TV drama. The character's face is pinned as though under a microscope for the viewer's close inspection. Although far from film size, the scale of the face intensifies responses in the TV close-up. Reaction shots frame the non-speaking actor, who listens and telegraphs feelings about what is going on. The two-shot, a device that emphasizes the effect of one character on another, is especially prevalent in TV drama. The elaborate use of a dramatic musical score, isolated shots of props and point-of-view shots extend the symbology of the dramatic material and heighten its power for the viewer.

The actor is under a video microscope in TV drama. The performer has to function inside these formal and thematic conventions to make them work for the characterization. A close-up of a hand, picking up a coffee cup or stubbing out a cigarette, may be the climax of a dramatic unit; a finger tapping on a glass may be the strongest statement of character the actor gets to make.

Soap characters (like those in most TV drama; the differences are mainly quantitative) are usually in transition. A strong subtext is crucial, since *secrets* and *withheld information* are basic plot devices. In continuing drama, very little is ever resolved—actors rarely get to finish an objective, complete a gesture, say an entire line as a complete sentence. The surface dialogue is often banal in the extreme, but it is played with total commitment to a full characterization with a specific career. The soap rhythm is usually slow: shots are held into long dissolves unless a brief climax is used to hype feelings with rapid cutting. A simple vocabulary of feeling-related gestures (*e.g.*, squinting with pain, eye-shifting for tense evasion and so on) creates the moment-to-moment action.

A soap acting style must be based in the formal style of the production itself. If the close-up and the tight two-shot is the major form for creating the action, the performer must work from a very few controlled facial gestures. Body work is secondary and is mainly used to support the face. Reactions must be strong and clear. Inner monologue can never stop, so that the actor is constantly *extending* and *illustrating* the action in the script in responsive silences.

Conversation is at the heart of the soap. The actor has to use conversational rhythm—the flow of talking and listening—to give the camera and the viewer every possible nuance of the subtext (soap characters have endless secrets kept from each other but not from the audience). This rhythm is slower in soaps than in the other genres discussed here. Dissolves and slow pans give the actor more time and more fluidity to establish reactions and responses. Since neither the text nor the action is ever defined or resolved, the actor must always refer to the *unseen*, remind us of the *absent*, the *unknown*. Sentences and phrases trail off, eyes drift away from the camera and from other faces. Every gesture, every inflection is pregnant with unspecified meaning.

In the soap genre, intentions are frustrated, undermined; character objectives are futile and empty. Suffering is at the heart of most soap scripts. The actor has to let us in on this pain and anguish while putting a good face on it for everyone else. There is a constant tension between the inside (the pain, the secrets) and the outside (the coping, the struggle). The direct objective of the performance is to reveal this tension clearly, to sculpt the character's career with it.

As indicated above, TV drama is a close relative of the soap and shares most of its stylistic performance requirements. "Drama" is used generally here to refer to any script that focuses on character and conflict. TV dramas are often linked to other genres, especially action shows and sit-com. The television-made movie is usually part of this genre, as is the PBS continuing dramatic series. Each subdivision and specialization of the TV drama has its own particular considerations; in general, all share a strong emphasis on people in conflict undergoing transition. The actor should follow the general characteristics of the soap style and adapt them to the special qualities of the material.

NON-BROADCAST TELEVISION PROGRAMMING

Non-broadcast video borrows from broadcast TV genres, especially from dramatizations. The rapid growth of institutional, community, non-profit, educational and industrial video is bringing about the creation of genre and style mixes that are new to TV viewers.

Non-broadcast video has been used most extensively to produce training and information tapes. The medical field has been using video since the 1950's, and for many years it was the major market for non-broadcast TV equipment. Medical training provides an example of the simplest kind of videotape produced for training. Physical modeling, or showing how to do something, is accomplished more successfully and effectively (especially in terms of cost) through video than any other medium. One typical example is the tape that shows a nursing student how to give an injection. The visual image imprints itself on the mind and has an effect that lectures, demonstrations and textbooks do not.

Documentary production, recording a real nurse as she gives an injection, is one way of making this tape. In most cases, however, the nurse has to be directed to "act" for the camera. In the same way that the actor in advertising cannot obscure the product, the nurse has to be able to demonstrate the activity clearly, with the TV screen in mind.

Documentary recording of physical modeling is a directorial problem that often is better solved by using actors who respond to the demands of the production process. Portable production and more flexible video-editing equipment will make the documentary approach attractive in some cases where the actor could not be expected to master the skills of the worker in the field. But, in fact, many "how-to" tapes are made to demonstrate relatively simple tasks, such as how to fill out a form. More and more of these tapes are being made with experienced actors, who can control the quality of the performance and deal with the point of the material: to explain.

The use of actors is definitely called for in a more complex kind of modeling tape—the tape that shows its viewers how to *be,* and to *interact* with other people. Video's live quality, discussed in Chapter 2, lends itself to modeling that demonstrates such interactions as the personnel interview. In this kind of tape, the personnel worker responsible for hiring learns how to question an applicant for a job. This use of modeling has become a part of all corporate management training. Tapes are also used to show union officials how to negotiate labor contracts, shop stewards how to argue in a grievance procedure, research interviewers how to ask questions without showing their own bias, secretaries how to answer the phone, doctors how to probe a patient's history, parents how to treat their babies.

In these modeling tapes, the development of character is not as critical to the actor as the understanding of the content and its subsequent demonstration. A natural video style is demanded; stagey acting destroys the intent of modeling. In one set of research interviewer training tapes, it was important that the tapes present a full range of non-college-educated types—young, old, black, white—who were the target of the training. The characters had to be individualized enough by the actors to prove that very different people could learn the same techniques and apply them, in spite of their differences. The actors had to demonstrate what not to do, playing interviewers and the respondents; in some cases, the actors were trained as interviewers and given non-actors to interview. This particular tape had a "teaser" or comic vignette to introduce it, to relax the audience; the vignette was a straight comedy skit, shot on location at a house with a two-camera system. This tape also included narrative portions with the actor talking directly to the viewer, summing up one example or leading into another. The tape contained a whole range of performance problems—and stylistic differences—for the actor.

The information tape has traditionally been treated as an illustrated lecture, but video directors are now beginning to use trained actors as such work reaches new audiences with more varied content. For example, another research-related tape was made to report on the results of a national study of children's achievement in school. This tape used actors to play both the children and the interviewer, to present the most common kinds of answers to key questions for each category of child, according to class, race, sex and age. Another tape, used in welfare office waiting rooms, explains the welfare regulations by showing someone finding his or her way through the bureaucracy.

In some cases, specialized information tapes will demand full characterization work. A recent tape made to explain a government-supported-work program featured vignettes with actors playing ex convicts. The tape was shot on location at job sites, where the characters talked to the camera about the workings of the program that placed them in the job and helped them stay there. The ex-con, ex-drug addict, welfare mother, black teenager, those who find jobs most difficult to get and hold, had to be portrayed more realistically than they've ever been presented on broadcast television because the specialized audience knew the difference. A detailed, almost documentary acting style was needed.

Many of the stylistic suggestions made for broadcast TV drama will also apply generally to dramatic non-broadcast videotape work. Because this kind of work often has a strongly documentary quality and intent, intense performances of the soap vein may be inappropriate. The clarity and commitment of performance is the same, but the performance intention changes. Conveying the information contained in the script has first priority; creating believable people is a necessary means to this end. Episodes are brief, and characters must be created quickly. Scripting is often not very clear on character, so the performer often must supply the definition on camera. Usually the goal is to create characters that the specialized viewing audience can easily identify with, characters that are similar to themselves and the people they work and live with. A little research and some time spent with the sponsor's employees and/or clients will give the actor a picture of the kind of person appropriate in the project.

SIT-COM

Unlike the soap and the TV drama, the purpose of the situation comedy is strictly to entertain and amuse. Character on sit-com is a secondary consideration. Characters are often two-dimensional and without much of an emotional life. Pain is the opposite of comedy; if the viewer becomes involved or concerned with the fate of the character, laughter disappears. Plot is usually drawn from one of a surprisingly small number of formulas. The situation is resolved cleanly and quickly, never really leaving us worried about the inevitable happy/celebratory ending.

Situation is everything in sit-com. Scripting and camera blocking set up the complications and imbalances of the comic situation; the actors are then free to unravel the story line with maximum emphasis on the incongruous, the unmasking of pretense, comic repetition and de-humanized behavior. Feelings and character careers exist mainly to further the situation and add to the comic action. Everything always comes out okay; the action concludes in a celebration of this primal comedic truth.

There is a basic stylistic difference between comedy and drama that is crucial to the actor: comedy is public, whereas drama can be private. Most sit-coms are either shot before live audiences or are doctored with recorded laugh tracks to appear as if they are. Viewers need to be part of the crowd in comedy, to join in with the rest of the public to really laugh freely. Sit-com without audible laughter on the audio track has rarely been successful in the broadcast media. Soap and TV drama, however, require the illusion of privacy, of intimacy. Scenes are usually set indoors, in small rooms. There is nothing absurd about having the pain and pathos there in the room with us, to be eavesdropped on alone. Sit-com, on the contrary, plays to a much larger generalized audience, which is acknowledged: we can hear the others laughing with us.

For the actor, sit-com performance style is broad, frontal, gener-alized. Even in an interior set, the cameras hold back for the medium shot that takes in the *situation* rather than the individual. Close-ups are rare, usually reserved for a quick and predictable reaction shot done straight into the lens to punctuate a gag. Accordingly, the scale of performance is broader and larger. Blocking is active, so that the entire set space is incorporated into the situation—people run, fall, crawl over the furniture, pop in and out of doors. Gestures are large and involve much more of the body than the face.

Since a live audience is either actually present or suggested, performance must acknowledge this extra reality beyond the camera, and the actor must play to a much larger area. Performance becomes frontal; the actor works for a 180-degree plane, of which the camera is just one part. Gestures, business, reactions are not revealed selectively to the camera (as in soap); instead, they are telegraphed broadly to the furthest corner of the studio and the last row of the auditorium. Reactions are generalized broadly: not a raised eyebrow to indicate surprise, but rather, both hands in the air, the jaw dropped, a huge intake of breath and a step backwards. The scale—medium or long shot—prevents the recorded image from seeming grotesquely overdone.

Unlike film, videotape is cheap. Many sit-coms (especially Lear shows, such as *All in the Family*) are shot with four or five cameras recording straight through, without breaks or repeated takes. A theatrical style that pays little attention to the camera is possible in this kind of shooting. Since several full takes are edited together for the best possible version, the actor can pull out all the stops and play to the general studio audience. Other shows are shot film-style, with each shot set up separately and shot until perfect. Here, the camera is still controlling the acting technique.

Distance may be the best term for a sit-com style. The camera, the audience, even the performer keeps back and away from much real human contact with the characters. The characters themselves react to the *situation* (a secret, a joke, mistaken identity) rather than to each other. Set the situation aright and they're all right as well; empathy with feelings is unnecessary, since the outcome is controlled externally and everything operates on the outside anyway. The viewer, the audience, the camera and the actor are free to stand back and enjoy the silliness together, without risk of feeling or involvement.

Characters developed for sit-com should be simple and direct. Character objectives are not an overriding concern; sit-com characters have attitudes rather than a full psychology. The actor should start with a *stance*, a posture toward the world that indicates what he or she expects from it. Stance can be derived from the body work described in Chapter 13. A fixed center of energy pinpoints the stance actively. Archie Bunker, for example, was built from the domelike forehead and fixed jaw of Carroll O'Connor. Archie meets things "head-on," but he often beats his head against the wall. Frustration and stubbornness are locked into the underslung jaw. The dangling arms and protruding belly give us the image of a defeated bull or bear, befuddled and angry about always getting the short end of things.

Image work helps to make the physical characterization of sit-com vivid and immediately recognizable. The viewer wants to get on with the jokes; there is no time for figuring out who people are and where they are coming from. The actor must present a physical character with its attitudes and expectations built in and apparent on the surface. The action of the story will trigger reactions like relays. Surprises and intimate revelations are not appropriate to sit-com characters; the physical image should tell us all we need to know.

The actor may have a clear character objective in the script, but this objective must not dominate the performance. The performance intention has to dominate: to amuse and entertain. Mary Tyler Moore (a master of the sit-com genre) may have to tell Lou Grant she is quitting, but only to make us laugh in the next scene over her "wishy-washiness." The performer who "gets into" Mary's need for independence and self-dignity as an objective will get lost in psychology and so miss the point of the work. Mary's frown is an upside-down smile that we *know* cannot ever be far away.

Objectives should be used technically in sit-com to help build the rhythm and timing of the scene. Comic timing, established in the structure of builds in the script and the pattern of the editing and cutting, is the core of the performance. The payoff is the laugh reaction of the audience. The actor joins in the general structure of this rhythm by placing the character in the comic action pattern. You should look at the script as a series of builds and payoffs, and see exactly how your character furthers this pattern. The payoffs are generally quick and immediate: one-liners are rapidly setup and climaxed, scenes are short, the entire script typically resolves the situation in twenty-four minutes of action. Objectives should be simple and immediate, based in the actual comic situation rather than beyond it. Each facet of the objective should move toward a resolution of the situation.

Because sit-com is so technically precise, it is usually blocked and rehearsed with extreme meticulousness. Timing on business blocking and prop use is crucial. This necessitates tremendous concentration and precision, as well as a feel for audience response. Sit-com style may require the greatest control over the actor's performance of any TV genre. The performer must be extremely clear on the planning and timing of every detail of the action. Ironically, the broader the style, the greater the control needed to carry off the effect.

The variety show—including stand-up comedy, skits and musical numbers—fits many of the stylistic requirements of sit-com. Performance is adjusted to the live audience. The interchange between performer and audience provides the rhythm of the performance. Audience response (clapping, laughter, cheering, silence) provides the punctuation for each unit in each section. The action is focused frontally and played broadly, using physical imagery and a broad repertory of large, stylized gestures. The performer should work non-psychologically for effects that are immediately recognizable, that have a quick payoff in audience response.

On the other hand, the Variety show performance is really developed for, and controlled by, the camera. The live audience—actual or simulated—is merely a stylistic device that frames the performance. The performance scale that is appropriate is one that suits the camera, not the last row in the auditorium. The studio audience gives the performer a focus and reference point, but the performance is actually designed for the TV viewer.

So many variations exist on the basic sit-com pattern that the pure form is actually rare. Elements of drama and soap are combined with sit-com to create many "family" shows like *The Brady Bunch, My Three Sons,* or *Little House on the Prairie.* This particular mixture of genres is difficult for the actor; the technical objectivity needed for comedy makes dramatic characters wooden and flat, and the empathy required for dramatic characters robs the comedy of its wit. Such productions are rarely either funny or involving.

Some sit-com variations develop their own distinct style and set of conventions. Norman Lear's actors burlesqued other genres in *Mary Hartman, Mary Hartman* and *Fernwood 2-Nite;* the distinctive style developed by the producer and director carried through to the acting and allowed the material to be developed on its own terms. NBC's *Weekend* and *Saturday Night Live* also mix genres freely, with uneven but usually original results. In such situations, the performer can rely on the creative personnel to establish the style and context of the performances. As long as comic intention is clear in performance, the actor can design a performance that will suit the stylistic reference sought by the producer and director.

ACTION SHOWS

The basis of the action show is movement. Cars speed through chases, the story flips from one twist to the next, characters pursue clues and each other, the camera jump-cuts from props to faces to moving objects. The actor is on the same level with the prop: another surface/object to be played off against in rapid sequence, with a quick definition. The action character is simply one more device to be manipulated within the conventions of the show, along with a hat, a gun, a car, a horse, a chase. Plots are reduced to rudimentary scenarios. What happens to whom is not as important as *how* it happens, the *way* it is done. Style in the action genre is defined by the way action is presented.

Acting for an action show requires a clear understanding of the conventions that are used to achieve action effects. In general, the video action image is sharp, brief and quickly defined. Characterizations must operate the same way. Character objectives need to be defined in strongly active, movement-oriented terms. The actor must start with a simple statement of what, as the character, he wants to *get*, to *do*. The action objective will provide the basis for a physical image that is simple and vivid and that relates to motion. Revenge, for example, as a character objective, will help to create a mask of anger for the face, a rigid shoulder and arm set and a way of handling hands and fingers (knotted, clawlike). The physical body and imagery used by the actor must carry a strong, immediate impact that the camera can convey in short, close-in shots. Rapid cutting to other objects and performers sets up quick contrasts and balances, weaving the actor into a mosaic of vivid, simplified images.

The action show on TV is heavily visual. Police and spy shows in particular use very little spoken dialogue; the camera does most of the work. Most successful continuing programs have a fixed style of directing and editing that carries from show to show, creating a strict set of visual conventions that the actor must work within. *Kojak*, for example, presents a series of vivid images for Telly Savalas by constantly framing his massive head against strong vertical and horizontal lines: hat brims, car windows and windshields, door frames. When you add a simple character device such as Kojak's lollipop, plus a mannered, gravelly voice and stark face lighting, Savalas's work as an actor is nearly all done before his performance begins. The actor must often work within such strict conventions, conventions that largely shape and complete the performance.

Performing in the action genre is similar to TV drama acting. The camera carries a point-of-view about the characters and the story, which is thus imposed by the angle, sequence and cutting rhythm of the shots. The actor needs to know, whenever possible, how the point-of-view is going to be handled on a shot-by-shot basis. The reactions and responses that create the role are secondary to what the camera actually shows the audience. Cutting from a mutilated body to Kojak's smile, or vice versa, tells the audience something about the character at that point. The actor's job is much simpler if he can control his responses based on the actual point-of-view that the director is developing.

The fixed conventions of the action genre mean that the actors control a much smaller portion of their performance. While it is important for the actor to have a strong grasp of the script, as well as the director's treatment of it, the actual performance must be handled on a much simpler, more immediate basis. A good starting point is the actual time units the script will be shot in. Action shows tend to work in short shots with rapid cutting. Actors are rarely held for more than one line, or one brief reaction to a piece of dialogue or action. The actor must master this kind of working rhythm, where a great deal must be achieved in a brief image. Working in one-liners means that each line is its own unit, finished and punctuated by the time the camera cuts away. A physical image should accompany each time unit, creating a strong statement of the character's attitudes about the situation for that moment.

Subtext must be conveyed by the body, vividly and quickly. Character interactions are usually handled in tight close-up, so small head and facial gestures and eye movements will carry much of the subtext. Movement and action—especially fights and chases—are usually recorded with medium to long shots, requiring the actor to make a clear attitude statement with whole-body stance and gestures. Obviously nothing very complex can be handled in one-second cuttings or long-distance movement sequences. The actor should work from the basic text and subtext message, leaving the director and editors to add shadings and depth with angles, lighting and cutting.

Even though the action show is primarily visual, much of the tone and viewpoint of the material is handled through sound. The musical scoring of the action show is a highly developed and specialized art. Music and sound-track elements have an enormous impact on how the action is perceived and interpreted; to prove this, simply turn the sound off for any police action show. Obviously the actor cannot base a performance in the audio score. Whenever possible, however, the actor should try to discover production plans for music and sound. Performance rhythms can be adjusted to use the audio level for contrast or for reinforcement of the acting.

Made-for-TV movies, heavily based in the action genre, leave more room for a creative approach to character business and detail work. Line delivery in these one-shot projects is less likely to be a fixed pattern and rhythm, which is a feature of the continuing program. Depending on the material and the directorial approach, the actor can adapt any of the stylistic suggestions given above to the circumstances of the performance. Genre elements are usually a very obvious part of the TV movie, and the performer needs to respect genre acting requirements as an integral part of the style of the material.

NEWS AND INFORMATION SHOWS

Because they deal with facts and current events, news and information programs seem to be free of style and genre considerations. Such programs have a very deliberate style, however, that is at the heart of how they work. News and information programming, from the talk show to the panel interview to the evening newscast, is completely styled and controlled in all phases of production. Performers in this kind of programming are actors giving a performance. Genre and style considerations are crucial to the effectiveness of the performance they give.

News and information shows share on common style—they are presentational in that they acknowledge that the viewing audience is actually there. The presence of the audience focuses the performance and gives it a definable quality—an intimacy that includes the viewer in an immediate, serious conversation/discussion. All available video resources are used to shape the news/information style: full-front blocking, close-in camera work, elaborate teleprompters, specialized set design and lighting. The actor is the focus of all these elements, the actor and the person that all that news is shared with—the viewer.

Performance on news/information programming can be dealt with like any other specialized acting style. The performer's primary objective is really a character objective, since the actor creates a definable character on camera. The performance objective for news/information does not have to do with the news itself or any scripted material; instead, the objective has to do with the person of the performer. What the performer must put across is his or her own sincerity, honesty, probity.

The traditional term for the kind of "moral character" peddled by the newscaster or announcer is *ethos*. The effectiveness of this sales job is extremely important. The actor must convince us that his or her ethos is one of honor, virtue, integrity, that he or she cares about our well-being. The news or information is secondary to the ethos of the announcer. The performer's sense of integrity and concern provides the viewer with security and reassurance despite the content of the news itself. The viewer, we assume, takes the news better from someone he or she can trust.

The second objective of the news/information performer is to create a sense of occasion. The material being presented may not be particularly significant, but the *occasion* must be. The performer's measured rhythm, gravity of tone, occasional wry humor, balanced against an essential seriousness of purpose—all such performance techniques combine to make nearly anything announced sound important. Walter Cronkite is the occasion, not the trivial happenings in the news. Considering how nearly Olympian Cronkite's ethos is, his performance objective is simply to remind us that his very speaking to us is important. What he actually says, the clips and reports he shows to the viewers, become important by association. Cronkite sells Cronkite, the news merely tags along. Cronkite is the occasion, the news is the excuse.

Because of the objective presentational style of news/information programming, individual performance styles are somewhat personal to the actual performer. The performer must develop his or her own ethos on an individual basis. The performance image, as previously discussed, is an extension of the personality of the performer. The actor needs to root the image of honor, concern, integrity, maturity, in those sides of himself that look most like the real thing. Often this image can be developed from a close older relative who stood for the appropriate ethos: grandfather, uncle, possibly a professor or minister. Voice pitch, rhythm, eye contact, even style of humor can be simplified and specified from these models to make a strong ethos for performance purposes.

Certain techniques are shaped by most news/information performers who have developed an appropriate style. Most are based in the requirements of the genre itself. First of all, camera work and cutting rhythm favors a medium shot, one-half to full body, held for the length of two to three sentences. This is a much longer basic time unit than the other genres we have discussed. Thus the basic performance rhythm of news/information programming tends to be slow. Pauses and breaks are used to build tension and add emphasis, especially toward the end of a particular sequence of material.

The crucial realization for any performer working in this style is that emphasis and interest is developed for the *performer*, not the *material*. Tension has nothing to do with the material (which is usually so abbreviated and "objective" as to be bland), only with the performance. Pauses and eye contact with the viewer are not used to make points but merely to heighten interest in the performer and his delivery. The message is "Believe *me*, listen to *me*," not "Believe what I say."

The news/information performer must build and hold interest during the entire length of the program, not just within the story or section. Thus the performer has a "career" as discussed above (see Chapter 13). This career exists apart from the news itself, which may be horrible, unsavory, depressing. The performer does not identify with the material, but with the viewer. Without the concrete character and plot of the other genres, the actor has to capture the viewer's interest, build it to some sort of climax near the end of the program and complete this energy cycle with a departure.

The news/information performer works with smaller units—such as the story or single interview—and builds through them to the end of the show. The stress and emphasis used for delivery is a pattern developed for audience interest alone. The well-trained performer's delivery rhythm has little to do with what the story means. Words are stressed arbitrarily, regardless of their sense, to create a pleasing pattern of rising interest throughout the story. Pauses and downward inflections occur where they sound good, not where they mean anything. Gibberish spoken in the same rhythm would sound meaningful and interesting. The individual story unit is finished off with its own climax and conclusion punctuated with eye contact with the viewer as well as an out-of-focus pause (*i.e.*, eyes away from the camera and on the script or notes) to allow the sense of significance to emerge.

The energy level of the next beginning, the next "attack" on the material, continues to build until the end of the program. In this way, the performer increases the viewer's interest response gradually, peaking at the end of the show and relaxing into a good-bye. Then, during the credits, the camera pulls back to break the illusion, revealing the studio and the entire apparatus that supported the ethos of the announcer. The illusion is broken, and the viewer is released from the tight focus and escalating energy of the broadcast by the neutral glamour of backstage.

This performance style also requires a tight and controlled relationship with the camera. Because the style uses the presentational convention of direct address, the performer must constantly confront and acknowledge the viewer. Focus on the camera creates the illusion of close rapport. A teleprompter is often placed over the camera lens in many studios, allowing the actor to read while staying with the viewer. Some practice is required or a kind of spacey myopia can result.

What must be preserved at all costs is the sense of rapport with the individual in the viewing audience. Each individual viewer is let in on a serious discussion, is privy to an important personal conversation about real things. Creating a sense of sharing, of letting you in on a quiet piece of the action is the heart of the performer's job. The camera becomes the surrogate for the patient, the client, the family member, to be informed and advised in a human, direct way. Performing in this style is one to one, close and immediate.

The various visual-aid paraphernalia so dear to news/information programming, such as maps and still pictures done on rear-screen projection, film clips, and location reports, all exist to support the performance of the announcer. Notice that none of these are placed in the plane or picture with the performer; they are around or behind or above, but never on the same level. All such devices exist to frame the performer, to support his ethos and his rapport with the viewer. The actor never turns away fully from the frontal plane and the camera, even to talk to an interviewee or another announcer. The focus is frontal, and the performer turns from the viewer only to share the other image briefly.

It is ironic that, of all the genres we have discussed, news and information programming is so fully *about* the actor. Much more so than in soaps, sit-coms or action shows, the performer dominates the news/information program with a mixture of personal image and delivery techniques. By acknowledging the audience, the performer is able to directly claim and manipulate the viewer's attention entirely separate from the material he or she presents. News/information performing style is a highly cultivated and specialized approach to acting.

COMMERCIALS AND PUBLIC SERVICE ANNOUNCEMENTS

The major characteristic of the commercial or public service announcement (PSA) is its briefness. Messages are rarely more than a minute, and are usually thirty seconds or shorter. A tremendous amount of information is packed into that time. Shots tend to be quick and short, with the basic time unit only a few seconds. Actors need a rapid, clear delivery and tremendous precision with gesture, prop handling, blocking and physical image. The time framework is so tight that rhythms must be exact, controllable and repeatable.

The point of a commercial or PSA is to get a specific response from a large segment of the viewing audience. The performer's objective is to draw that response, using the material, from the viewer. In order to work effectively within such tight limitations, the actor has to base his or her work on several concrete decisions. What is the exact character or personality image to be presented? What is the performer's relationship to the product (or information)? What is the performer's relationship to the audience?

Commercial work is not superficial, even though the finished product is brief and the subject may not be edifying (*e.g.,* a drain cleaner). Instead, it is *compressed.* The character or personality created for the spot should have a career—some change from beginning to end that involves wanting or getting something. This career needs to have smaller steps, broken down by the shot sequence of the script. A clear beginning, middle and end should be kept in mind, no matter how the material is shot. Gestures, business, mannerism—all need to be simplified and condensed to make a strong impression with two or three devices.

The product—which may also be the information in a PSA—is the heart of the commercial. In order to put it across, the performer must have a clear relationship to it: it saved his life (smoke detector), it made him sexy and appealing (after-shave), it gives class by association (symphony season subscriptions). Straight information PSA's are handled like news and information programming; the performer sells his or her own ethos and charm first, using the material as a vehicle.

In any case, a clear relationship to the product or its symbol is absolutely essential. The performer's attitude about the product tells the viewer what to think about it. If the performer actually handles the product, it should be treated as something very special. The actor has to relate to the product and the audience at the same time, neglecting neither. The brand name must be kept visible and the object placed in a good position to be seen.

Most characters and personality images in commercials have a relationship with the viewing audience already spelled out in the material. The performer may be the expert, the friendly neighbor, an older relative or authority figure or a sexy seductive love-object. The performer acts out this audience relationship directly—by full camera address to the viewer at the end or at the beginning of the message—or indirectly—by the way he or she deals with the audience stand-in character in a dramatization.

The basis of the performer/audience relationship in a spot is usually authority and empathy. The performer lets us know that he or she understands the situation and our needs and that he or she really cares enough to give us what we need, whether we know it or not. The performer has to keep the audience in mind at all times, to develop some kind of clear attitude about the viewer that ties him into the product as well. The performer's image, the product and the audience constitute an active triangle that the actor has to keep fully alive in performance.

The actual structure of the commercial will, of course, depend on the model used by the creators. The actor should determine what the genre model is and base the performance in the conventions that apply to the material. Sit-com is one of the most common models used for commercials, but nearly anything else may be used: documentary, police action and so on. The point is to make the commercial look like the show, only more intense and vivid. Condensation and reduction of effects into simple, workable business is the basis of a "spot" acting style.

GENERAL ISSUES IN TV PERFORMANCE STYLE

Continuing Characters

Actors doing any type of series have a special set of problems in creating and sustaining a continuing character. The character must be interesting enough to hold the viewer's attention again and again, under all sorts of circumstances. The character must have enough variety to hold up in repetition, yet have a clear enough core to provide continuity within the series. The acting challenges are enormous, and the rewards as well—repeating a character develops depth and statute in any performer's work.

The starting point for any continuing character is an understanding of her or his place in the general scheme of the show. Stooge, sidekick, comic maid, straight-man to the wise-cracker, simple-minded ingenue— the basic situation of the show will have a formula role for each character. The writers and director will ordinarily make this role clear in the treatment and in rehearsal. The actor's job is to personalize the formula, to develop a general character objective that accounts for the character's usual function in the script. The cop's partner may have to be right, may need to be correct all the time—making him the brittle foil who is aloofly superior to everyone. The typical plot may involve humbling him at least once an episode, proving that he shares other people's humanity.

Since some basic variety is needed to sustain a series, continuing characters will be subjected to a range of experiences that may have little to do with the character's general objective. To sustain the character, the actor would do well to make the objective into a *stance,* an attitude toward the world that indicates what the character expects out of life. Archie Bunker clearly expects frustration and insult; his stance is aggressively defensive. Other stances can communicate confusion, reassurance, killing anger. Since characters are defined by whom they meet, the stance signals how they are likely to respond. A stance is a less psychological way of creating a quick, vivid profile that a character can act out with infinite variation, in repeatable and recognizable patterns.

A clear physical body can be developed from the character's stance by making the posture a literal expression of this basic attitude. The posture is a complete set of physical attitudes, from hair style to weight and foot placement. Body posture must be recognizable under any costume, set or lighting conditions. A set posture is a direct statement of continuity from moment to moment, episode to episode.

The usual action pattern in a continuing script has the central characters somehow disrupted from their usual relationship by a surprising change in circumstances. The conclusion shows them restored to their original way of being. Each character needs a regular way of responding to the disruption and restoration. This response to change is a signature, an identifying device that indicates the character's fundamental beliefs about the world. Archie Bunker is indignant and self-righteous, mugging wildly to indicate his basic belief in the world's predictable idiocy. Walter Cronkite is patient and somber, his face cocked to one side in a wry indication of the inevitable helplessness we all share. Telly Savalas freezes in untouchable imperturbability; nothing can move that massive strength.

The signature response helps the character continue and support the world of the series. Stance and a limited vocabulary of gestures and manners provide other familiar tools to meet a given week's brand of the unknown. The actor's repertory of business is deliberately limited for the continuing character. The very familiarity of the response reaffirms the solidity of the world, no matter what the change. We know who these people are and we know what they will do, no matter how improbable the circumstances become. The actor holds the series together by continuing the character as a predictable fact in a changing universe.

Presentational vs. Representational Performing

The kind of audience the actor works for—and where this audience is placed—is a major determinant of performance style for TV. The possibilities form a continuum, from the strict illusion of the soap to the semi-documentary direct-camera delivery of a location report. The actor and the camera place the audience and set up the audience's response to the material. The style of dealing with the audience, as we have seen above, determines the style that the actor works within.

TV drama and soap opera are closest to the traditional theatre. There is an unseen wall, behind which an audience spies on the characters. The camera is a kind of keyhole that lets the viewer peep in at the action. The actors acknowledge neither the audience nor the camera. They are their own audience, watching themselves and each other undergo excruciating personal discomfort. The actor uses the character to *disclose,* to reveal the nuances of the unspoken, the unconscious. The audience is composed of near voyeurs, erotically violating the illusion of privacy that the keyhole creates. The actor responds in kind by teasing, tantalizing, revealing in hints and suggestions, with detail and inflection. The camera is the unseen lover, the uncaring god, the invisible persecutor. The performer unveils for the camera in slow motion, a detail at a time. The acting style is psychological, sensual, inherently artificial.

Action shows implicitly admit the camera into the scene. The camera creates the action and gives the motion that moves things along. The camera is outside, above the struggle, or a part of the rapidly moving machinery that rolls it along. The actor is merely another object to the indifferent eyes of the lens. Victims are natural in action shows, as the actor helplessly faces the gun/camera without protection. The actor is pinned, trapped, nailed by the ruthless eye of the action. Responses are sharp, unmasked, rapid. The audience is a part of the camera and is rushed through the action along with it. The acting style is brutal, direct, abbreviated.

Sit-com and variety shows acknowledge the camera as one more part of the live audience that is out there watching the show. The camera is mounted on the line that slices this circular world into two halves: set and actors on one side, audience and home viewers on the other. The illusion (or the reality) of the live audience means that the actor also works for the broad frontal plane that the cameras sit on. To work frontally is to work generally and broadly. The actor must focus for the whole frontal plane rather than the specific point of the camera. The camera is more of a recording device and less of a point-of-view. The actor here does much of the work that the camera usually does in other performance styles. The actor's timing and pauses are slower, more direct, in place of editing and cutting. Climaxes are large and spread out for the whole audience to see. Business and gags are pointed out to everyone, rather than presented in tight focus to the single camera. The home viewing audience is in the front row, included in the general hilarity and good times. The acting style is large-scale, broad, non-specific.

Location and documentary work confront the camera directly and treat it as the eye of the audience. The viewer is invited in to see people and things in a natural state. The performer or announcer is free of most stylistic conventions, except for the illusion of the viewer's actual presence. The performer will usually establish a natural, direct relationship with props and objects in the immediate environment. The audience is present as the curious eye, examining whatever is pointed out. The acting style is direct, conversational, unmannered.

News and informational programming tends to disregard the camera and focus directly on the viewer. The camera is merely a window through which the announcer speaks to each individual in the audience. While the actor here works without a full character, an idealized image is projected of interest and concern in matters that affect the viewer. The performer works conversationally, as though he or she and the viewer were sharing the room together. Camera work is deliberate and unobtrusive, to preserve the illusion that the camera isn't really there—only the people are. Delivery is even and rhythmic, designed to generate attention and interest regardless of the material. The audience is welcomed directly, invited to participate. The acting style is direct, conversational, hypnotic.

Performance Objectives

The final factor to be considered in video performance style is probably the most important: the purpose and the objective of the performance itself. The performer must not only be clear on where the audience is and how to relate to them; he or she must be positive and settled about what kind of response is desired from the viewer. Reducing the issue crassly to its very basics, actors need to let the viewer know what they are selling. A good time? Laughs and entertainment? A story? A believable character? A product? Information? How sexy the performer him- or herself is? How bright/clever/knowledgeable he/she is? Usually a performer is selling a combination of the above. The priorities must be crystal clear, or the performance will be murky and hollow.

Generally, performance objectives stress either character/role values or entertainment values. Character/role work requires a great deal of detail and attention, as outlined above. Entertainment values, either in a variety skit or a dramatic action show, can also have priority in a performance. In this case, the actor will concentrate on much more technical considerations: rate and timing, relation to the camera, vivid and concrete gestures, climaxes and pauses and so on. While such considerations always apply generally, the performer's immediate priorities must be clear for the performance style to be valid and appropriate.

Similarly, the performer's relation to the material needs to be spelled out. Depending on the purpose of the performance, the performer may be the material itself (as in the news), a facilitator of the material (interviews, sportscasting) or a vehicle for the material (dramatic characters). The actor can control the distance between the self and the material, but what the audience is actually supposed to see has to be decided clearly. What is more important, the performer or the performance?

The actor's purpose in working will really shape and form the performance. The techniques of performance are a means; the end is a certain kind of response from the audience. The actor needs to keep that response in mind through every phase of planning and performing. Mugging, self-consciousness and rampant ego will drop away quickly if the relation between means and ends, between performance and audience, is kept constantly in mind.

SUMMARY

Styles of acting for TV are as varied as what ends up on the screen any day of the week. Non-commercial and non-broadcast video have many more uses that extend the work of the performer into whole new areas. In the best of all possible worlds, a TV actor would be free of the pressures of genre conventions anyway. Each production would develop its own style, based on the material and the input of all creative personnel, including actors.

In reality, however, everybody watches TV and shares the collective consciousness of actual TV practice. TV shows have developed their own vocabularies of gesture, delivery, characterization, blocking. These vocabularies are part of a gradually emerging television tradition that affects everyone who works with, and watches, TV.

The serious student of TV acting needs to watch a *lot* of TV without regard to the type or quality of the programs. Common conventions, such as Lucy's mugging or Kojak's squint, are not models or even fixed ways of working; instead, they are a language of gesture open to interpretation, innovation, improvisation. The actor may manipulate this material directly or indirectly in countless ways. The actor is no more limited than is his imagination.

In production, it is necessary to know as clearly as possible what conventions you are working under, what genre assumptions are or aren't operating. Often such stylistic concerns are assumed rather than stated, but you can discuss these issues with the director and the other actors. Finally, style comes from your attitude about the material you are working with. You can define this attitude for yourself and let your conclusions shape your performance.

Part Three

WORKING PRODUCTION —THE PERFORMER IN THE PROCESS

17

PERFORMING

The complex nature of TV as a medium creates a number of specific problems for the performer. Video work cannot easily be done without a large number of people doing highly specialized jobs. It is an expensive medium and a time-consuming one. The TV actor, unlike the stage actor, is a small component of the overall process.

Briefly, the most difficult problems the actor will usually encounter in TV performance are:

1. Multiple takes
2. Frequent interruptions
3. Physical proximity of crew
4. Lack of a silent work area
5. Last-minute changes in script
6. Reblocking during shooting
7. Lack of a sense of final product; no overall view of production
8. Physical restrictions because of cameras and microphones (*i.e.*, meeting marks and such)

WORKING IN THE STUDIO

The general layout of a studio, including the necessary people and equipment, is discussed in Chapters 7 and 8. Here let us simply note that even a small studio production usually requires a crew of six, plus a director and an assistant director; equipment includes at least two cameras, several microphones, a switching unit and sound mixer. The time required to set up, light and shoot a thirty-second spot (exclusive of pre-production time) may well be eight hours or more. There is generally no way to avoid such extensive time demands. Lighting requires considerable time and often must be reset for each angle. Multiple takes and frequent reblocking are necessities; the actor cannot work in the splendid, uninterrupted isolation of the stage or lecture platform.

Just as frequent interruptions are a fact of the medium, so is the noise and constant activity of the studio. With six or more people working on the floor at any given time, responding to instructions from the control booth, and trying to stay within time limits, silence is rare. So is physical isolation; generally the floor manager talking into his headset is nearby, maybe only three or four feet away, while an audio person may be holding a fishpole microphone only two or three feet away and following the performer's every move.

Often TV performers feel not only interrupted but unnoticed, ignored, or handled like puppets to be casually moved about. In comparison to the attention performers receive on stage, the apparent focus they receive in a studio may be minimal. Each member of the crew has a specific and isolated job to do. At times, the audio person may seem interested in nothing but concealing the microphone, the lighting person only in getting rid of the boom shadow. While such division of labor may be frustrating and make talent feel ignored, the goal is after all to make the performer look good. There is no way in TV that performers can "do it themselves." In the final analysis, all roles—from camera operator to performer—must be viewed as equally important.

WORKING WITH A DIRECTOR

Because of the complexity of the medium, the performer is working in a dependent situation and must be willing to accept restrictions and follow instructions. The relationship between the performer and director grows out of this situation.

A director and/or producer has pre-planned a production so that blocking is compatible with lights, cameras and microphones. The actor/performer is, for the most part, under far tighter restrictions than on stage. While the purpose and effect of each movement, the reason for each "mark," may be clear to the director, it is often little more than arbitrary to the actor. The freedom to, within limits, control one's own performance so often available on stage is gone. An actor in TV must accept two facts. First, he or she is dependent on the director to see the performance as it looks on the screen; second, the final product will be controlled by many things other than the work of the actor. What is shown, how much is shown, when it is shown and how the audience responds are all subject to the director's or producer's choices in the control room or editing room. A performer's special gestures may never be seen; sequences may be rearranged; music or laugh tracks may be added. It is often difficult, but generally necessary, to be able to follow instructions exactly, even when the logic behind them is not apparent.

TV directors are also interested in camera work, audio work and engineering problems as well as performance problems. While most directors will give the talent considerable attention, stage actors are often shocked to find out how much they must share the director's attention with the crew. If the show is to look good, a director must necessarily pay attention to many things besides the actor.

TV directors have a variety of working methods and come from a variety of backgrounds. Some expect actors to follow exact instructions, and they shoot in long—five to fifteen minute—segments; others give few instructions but shoot almost line by line, record on three or four cameras and then edit extensively in post-production. Many TV directors come from a technical media or journalism background, with little or no acting training themselves. As a result, they tend to direct actors very differently than a traditional stage director would. It is important for the performer to be adaptable to the working methods of the individual director. One director may speak clearly about objectives and characterization, another may only describe the effect he or she wants the performer to create. Some directors will give detailed criticism after each take; others will primarily focus on crew problems and rarely mention performance. Despite such differences in approach, each director is trying to make the 'talent,' and thus the production, effective. The performer who is focused on this same goal will usually take personal responsibility for his or her own performance.

ENERGY AND CONCENTRATION

Many performers find that the problems of TV performance drain their energy and badly disrupt their concentration. The TV studio or location seems almost as if some fiendish creature had designed the most disruptive, energy-draining and frustrating work environment imaginable. Once shooting begins, several different work patterns may occur, depending on the show being produced. Each pattern of work presents its own problems. Discussed below are three examples of the performance problems related to TV program styles.

In a serial or drama where each minute (or less) is shot separately, a flow to the performance is often difficult to achieve. Each of these takes is probably shot several times; not infrequently, as many as six to ten takes will occur. Often there is little or no break between the takes. The performer must be ready to go immediately. Ten takes without a break is exhausting to anyone.

To further drain the actor's energy, it may be thirty minutes or even two hours before he or she is needed on the set again. The next sequence he or she works in may well not be sequential to the previous work. Since all takes requiring a certain setup will be shot at the same time, without regard for chronology, concentration and energy in a serial or dramatic work cannot be obtained or sustained by continuity. The performer needs such a firm grasp on the plot and character that he or she can enter the story at any moment, without "building" to a particular scene.

In the format of a talk show, the performer may enter the studio two or three hours before the show, go over the scripted material, rehearse any opening or closing sequences, meet the guests and get into costume and makeup. The show is then probably shot straight through. One hour before a camera without a fixed script is an extremely demanding situation for the performer. The host cannot simply concentrate on the conversation. A number of commercial breaks must be taken. These breaks, signaled for by the floor manager, usually require a verbal lead-in—"and now we have a message"—and often a physical gesture or turn of the body from the host. These breaks must come at particular times no matter what the normal flow of the conversation. Thus, the host's concentration is always divided between the guests and the signals of the floor manager.

News shows, with their many segments—weather, feature stories, film clips, as well as commercials—are even more disjointed for the performer. Bound by strict time limits, the announcer/performer must concentrate on instantly beginning his or her own segment when the previous performer is finished, looking away at a film clip at exactly the right moment and covering each item in exactly the number of seconds allowed. All this must happen while the performer, surrounded by moving cameras and microphones, appears to talk directly to the home viewer. While information shows are often edited, there is little post-production time; pressure to do it right the first time and accomplish much of the editing in the control room is great.

Techniques to Save Energy and Keep Concentration

These situations discussed above are only examples of three possible working patterns. Many variations may arise. While each situation will present specific problems, some suggestions that should be generally useful can be made.

For Energy:

1. Conserve energy during rehearsals. In TV you will often be involved in a technical rehearsal, a rehearsal for camera and mi-

crophone, or kept on set for a light or audio check. Such rehearsals do not demand full performance energy. While a performer must never be "sloppy" in any rehearsal, you can choose to use only the amount of energy necessary for the specific task. The different types of rehearsals and the demands they make are discussed later in this chapter.

2. Exercises to relieve tension such as those suggested in Chapter 18 for warm-up work can be helpful during the work day. A "roll-down" or a "rotation" can be used in almost any short break.

3. Give up control. Many actors develop severe tension and use untold amounts of energy in "fighting the process," in trying to control, manage or speed up a given situation. No director or producer wants to waste time, no technician is likely to want a bad product, and, frankly, no beginning performer is going to change the way in which these people work. The best advice, then, is relax and "flow" with the process.

Flowing with the situation is much easier when a performer understands the media. While an in-depth knowledge of video technology is hardly necessary, the technical information given in Chapters 2, 3, 6, 7 and 8 will make the process seem less arbitrary.

4. Find your own way to "drop out." Tension is contagious, so plan for long waiting periods when you have nothing to do in the work situation—bring a novel, for example, or whatever you enjoy relaxing with.

For Concentration:

1. Learn to focus on small units of space and small segments of action. Be sure, for example, that you have clearly in mind the beginning, middle and end of the task to be performed in each take—even if it is nothing more than an entrance or exit.

2. Also, allow the lights and set to isolate areas of space for you. While you must be aware of the cameras and microphones, you can reduce the number of distractions by allowing people outside the set to fade into shadow for you. You need only to see the floor director.

3. Be well prepared with lines or with a clear memory of the sequences of events. The better you know your script and blocking, the less likely you are to be thrown off. Many well-trained actors have difficulty remembering lines in TV work. *Practice* entering the script at any point—logical or not—and running through one page of lines and blocking. *Learn* to visualize your blocking and to run through your lines in crowded and confused places, such as subway stops or on buses.

Most performers born after World War II already have many of the necessary concentration skills for TV work. The postwar generation has been raised to focus on more than one stimulus at a time without becoming exhausted or distracted. Many of us were raised to watch TV while doing homework, or to read with the stereo on at the same time. The TV studio, in this respect, is much like the modern home.

WORKING WITH A PARTNER

Sharing a Scene

A *shared scene* is a situation on camera in which actors appear to be genuinely listening, watching and reacting to one another. A "causal" relationship—you say/do something and it causes me to say/do something—seems to exist between them. Their feelings about one another, and the sense of their involvement with each other, show as clear and believable. When scenes are not shared, a viewer may well have the feeling that a character would continue on with a set performance even if the other character or characters were not there or never delivered their lines. The character and role work recommended in Chapters 13 and 14 will produce believable results in performance when actors genuinely share scenes with each other.

The shortage of rehearsal time, discontinuous shooting, the special blocking necessary for cameras and microphones and the need for multiple takes in TV work all present real barriers to shared performance work. You may have little or no time to rehearse with your partner; in order to be open to the camera, you might be blocked in such a way that you cannot even see your partner.

The interaction between you and another actor may be frequently interrupted. You might have a scene in which you must slap your partner, but the line that makes you angry is part of another take. The provoking line that actually motivates your action may have been shot thirty minutes before you perform the slapping scene. Occasionally you will have a sequence of lines to perform when your partner is not even in the studio. His or her reactions to your lines will be shot later and then the sequences edited together.

The work done in the editing can emphasize shots in such a way that actors will seem to be on set at the same time, appear to be talking to one another or looking at each other. Actors must be able to create an image of contact and involvement so that, in the final product, an interaction is not only physically apparent but is believable as well. Actors must be able to motivate directions that are primarily technical, finding reasons for each prescribed action that will emphasize their relationship and involvement in the scene.

Regrettably, actors often find that they can share well in the first or second or even third take. Later, after numerous takes, it is often hard to work with a partner spontaneously, moment to moment, and not merely perform the scene in a fixed pattern.

Below are some simple techniques that should help you share a scene successfully in spite of TV studio problems.

Before Shooting

1. Be sure that you and your partner are clear on the nature of your involvement (*i.e.,* the jealous mother and the dutiful daughter, the fearful citizen and the judge). Talk this relationship through so that there is no danger of misunderstanding how you each feel, as your character, about the other. Try to explore the relationship so that it is more than a stereotype. Why is the mother jealous? Why is the citizen fearful of the judge? If possible, discover one or two gestures that seem to epitomize the relationship—a clutching hug by the mother to which the daughter does not respond, or a bowed head and scolding finger. These gestures and body positions probably will not, in fact, be actually used in the shooting. Rather, they are symbols of the relationship. If you can physically demonstrate a relationship, you probably understand the attitudes underlying it.

2. With your partner, agree on a one-sentence statement of the objectives that you each must perform in the scene. The mother in the example above must convince the daughter not to leave home, while the daughter must insist on leaving without upsetting her mother. You should be able to state your objective in terms of your partner: "to prevent you from leaving home" or "to leave home without hurting you."

3. Run your lines with your partner, several times if possible, and try to maintain constant eye contact. Really see the other person.

4. Study your partner's physical appearance. Then try to describe your partner as if you were assisting a police artist in developing a portrait of him or her. Go right into your lines together when you finish.

5. Use the exercise in Chapter 14 in which you and your partner run your lines while tossing a light object back and forth between you. This exercise forces a genuine interaction to occur.

6. Run the subtext, the inner meaning of your lines, with your partner. At times it is easy to have developed incompatible subtexts independently of each other, and running this material together will clarify things. In period plays or stylized works, sharing can also be improved by paraphrasing the lines with your partner. Paraphrasing and subtext are explained in Chapter 14.

7. Talk through your blocking with your partner. Include the motivations you have found for the movements. For example:

    a. I cross to my center mark to be near you.

    b. I then move to my left (mark) because I don't want you to be near me.

    c. I stay on my mark but turn away from your because I am angry and want you to feel rejected.

    d. I cross to your mark to try to apologize to you. And so on.

During Shooting

1. Always be aware of your partner's body position. Even if you cannot see him or her, you should have a visual image of his/her placement on the set.

2. Listen to the lines as if you had never heard them before. Listen for new meanings in each take and respond to the way the line is actually delivered—not the way you heard it delivered in the last take.

3. Set a physical task in relationship to your partner at every moment. You might, for example:

    a. Try to maintain eye contact.

    b. Try to avoid eye contact.

    c. Listen to his/her walk.

    d. Listen to his/her breathing.

There are many possible tasks, and an appropriate one can be found. Such tasks, however simple, keep your focus on your partner, which is where it must be if a scene is shared.

4. If your partner is not in the studio, or if his or her segments of the scene are not being shot at the same time your section is, try to hear your partner's lines in your mind and to visualize him or her reacting to your lines. While this situation is difficult, the scene can seem shared particularly if you and your partner rehearsed the sequence beforehand. This situation is similar to the performance problem presented by a telephone conversation where the line is dead. The performer must, by concentration and detailed reactions, give the impression that he or she is involved in an actual conversation with a non-existent partner.

REHEARSALS

To prepare to actually tape or film a particular show, a number of different types of rehearsals will be held. Not all of the rehearsals described below will be used every time you work, but you will eventually be involved in most of them.

The rehearsal situation in TV is usually a surprise for the stage actor. Serials rarely rehearse more than four days, news shows may have only technical rehearsals, while commercials may be rehearsed and shot in the same day. Here, then, are the most common types of rehearsals.

Acting Rehearsals Off the Set

The cost of operating the studio facility makes it necessary to hold most beginning rehearsals elsewhere, away from the equipment and the organized chaos of the on-camera performing situation. The studio setting is usually simulated in size and scale on the bare stage of the rehearsal hall by a careful mapping out of dimensions and the arrangement of substitute furniture for doorways, chairs, tables. Hand props are often brought to the rehearsal hall and worked with, to anticipate specific handling problems that must finally be worked out in front of the camera.

Directors usually begin with line readings and characterization problems when working with performers and scripts in rehearsal. Many directors wish to have these issues pretty well settled before turning to more technical considerations. Performers tend to work much better with blocking, camera movement and shot size if they can be clearly motivated by the content and purpose of the program. Turning from camera 1 to camera 2 is easier if the actor can motivate a turn away from eye contact with another character and then open up in a two-shot to show the reaction. (Note the technical direction discussion below.)

The detailed requirements for complex blocking can be worked out without cameras by substituting a chair or the body of the director for a camera position. Once the performer has an understanding of the shot size and the camera being taken, it is possible to rehearse to scale. The director can then give feedback on the actor's use of the frame and relationship to other actors, as well as background and foreground properties in the shot.

Acting Rehearsals On the Set

Leaving the bare-stage rehearsal hall, the actors may get one or two rehearsals on the set in the TV studio without the presence of the crew. In this rehearsal they must become familiar with precise blocking and develop their own cues in relation to the setting. For example, an actor might say to himself, "When I turn away from her, I see the vase of flowers and step sideways, toward the left side of the couch." Thus the blocking becomes internalized, relating to the content and the setting.

Technical Rehearsals

The director usually conducts a technical rehearsal from the floor. The purpose of this rehearsal is to finalize camera shots and boom placement, while making sure the actors' gestures and prop handling actually fit the camera operators' frames. The director has the floor manager put down toe marks for the actors and floor marks for the cameras. Usually the director will not rehearse whole lines of dialogue. Instead, he or she will concentrate on the transitions from shot to shot. At this point, the director is concentrating on traffic and production technique questions, such as: is there time to move into the next shot, is there sufficient depth of field, does the operator understand that a certain prop has to fill a side of the screen? The technical run-through is usually a brisk rehearsal, without much concern for the actors, who are simply finalizing a technical relationship with the crew. Performers should not expect any response to their perfunctory performances at this point.

Final Run-Through From the Booth

The director will usually leave the finer questions of framing and the speed of camera movement—pan, tilt, dolly, the speed of the zoom—until a run-through from the control room. At this point, the floor manager, who has been absorbing all the director's decisions, becomes the director's representative in the studio; he or she sets up rehearsals and relates criticisms and adjustments from the director. In some cases, the director will use the studio announce system to address a direction out loud to the assembled crew and cast. This approach has the advantage of directness but gives little of the individual attention that can be carried by the floor manager.

The rehearsal from the booth is most often run straight through, with the director saving comments until after the scene is finished. Some directors, however, will work a stop-start rehearsal, solving each problem they see by asking the actors to freeze, and correcting positioning of cameras and cast shot by shot. Other directors save the problems, and will ask the FM to recreate a specific sequence of shots to work out framing and blocking. The FM will say, "We're going to re-block the line at the couch; places everybody; could you hold the cup up a little higher; that's it and look down when he says 'It's over;' thank you, standby, action . . . cut. Let's do it once more; give me a two-beat pause before you look down. Okay, standby, action. . . ."

Many video productions do not use the tool of video playback for rehearsal. However, the instant availability of what has just been taped is one of the tremendous advantages of video over film, especially in setting the precision of comedic timing, and in blocking exact movement and prop handling. With video tape, directors can finish certain that they have gotten a good take. In many cases, the director will want to quickly review a take during rehearsal, to critique it and to decide on minor adjustments of camera angle or lighting. Actors have to accommodate themselves to these playback periods, which are not for their benefit. They may be asked to stay in place waiting for the next take. There is always a compromise being made between time and money and bringing out the best in every production aspect. The talent has to learn to accept the rest of the crew's rehearsal requirements as well as his or her own.

MAKING TECHNICAL DIRECTIONS MEANINGFUL

In TV work, performers are often inundated with technical directions necessary for the camera, the lighting or the editing plan. We have already discussed many of these kinds of directions. A better performance results when the performer can somehow make these directions *more than* technical requirements.

One example of how to translate technical directions into motivation is given above in the exercise for sharing blocking with a partner. In that exercise, the actor connects *meeting marks* to character interrelationships in the script. In another situation, you might be asked to lean back slightly as your partner sits down so that you do not block her key light.

To translate this direction into motivated action, you might decide that you lean back because you are surprised by her sitting and must regain your composure, or you might decide that you must lean back to see her better.

Whenever you make a decision to motivate a technical direction, you want to be very sure that your choice is either indicated by the script or at least logical within the parameters of the script. It is never an actor's right to, on his own, change a script; bringing in motivation from beyond the script may well do so. Actors are ill-advised to decide that a character rises because he sees someone across the street or he has a leg cramp, for example, unless the script indicates such a choice. Even the simplest thirty-second spot will contain a number of possible motivations for nearly any technical direction without the actor having to bring in extraneous material.

Remembering the technical directions *exactly* is the actor's foremost concern. One director, a friend of the authors, is fond of telling about the performer who was fired because he could not remember to lean over the table at the correct moment to free another actor's light. After ten takes the director said, "I don't know why you can't lean like you're told to, but I don't have any more time to waste." Another actor got the job. With many directions for any given take, remembering is not always an easy task.

Not only must a performer remember all directions, but each one must be executed believably in the normal flow of the take. Any hesitation or self-consciousness with a given instruction may well be seen by the audience, destroying the integrity of your performance. While the personality performer occasionally acknowledges technical directions, the performer playing a dramatic role never does so. When a talk show host does reveal technical concerns, they are made a part of the show (for example, asking for a specific shot or telling a guest to look at the camera). Generally the directions necessary to get a show on tape should go unnoticed by the viewer.

In dramatic and situation comedy shows, technical adjustments must not only go unnoticed but, appear as a perfectly logical thing for the character to do. On the *Mary Tyler Moore Show,* Ted crosses away from Lou Grant *to look at a script* on Murray's desk, not *to clear the area* around Lou because the editing plan calls for a close-up of Lou. The former reason is the motivation; the latter reason is the need for it.

In the rush of TV production, it will generally be the actor's responsibility to translate directions to motivations. Such a performance skill can make the difference between mediocre performances and exciting ones, between days filled with retakes rather than successful takes, between being re-hired or used only once. One TV director recently told us that the ability to motivate necessary directions alone makes an actor worth more than scale.

18

WARM-UPS

Warm-ups are considered a necessity by most actor/performers just as they are by dancers and athletes. The warm-ups used by actors should do three things: 1) awaken and relax the physical body, 2) awaken and exercise the vocal mechanism and 3) put the performer in the proper state of mind and emotional posture to work.

Warm-ups do not substitute for daily work with a body/mind system, such as Yoga or T'ai Chi, or for the thorough study of the physical and vocal techniques of a serious theatre-training system. The bibliography at the back of the book contains a list of books that describe such systems. Warm-ups simply ready a trained body and voice or assist the beginning or occasional performer in getting the very most from himself or herself in a given situation.

Most trained actors have developed a warm-up system that they use regularly. For TV work, such a system (or any system that a beginning performer may choose) should be modified in two ways.

First, exercises used should emphasize relaxation. While exercises for physical fitness and strength are generally useful for health and conditioning, the studio performer should avoid strenuous calisthenics as a warm-up. Any physical tension—raised shoulders, tight face, locked jaw, clenched hands—is visible on camera; it restricts freedom of movement and changes vocal quality.

Second, a useful studio or location warm-up must be designed for limited space—the dressing room, an isolated corner or a hallway. The stage actor often has use of the full stage or at least a large space for a warm-up led by an acting coach or director. The TV actor will usually warm up alone between costume calls, makeup calls and voice level checks. Moreover, as his or her work will be interrupted many times, he or she may well need to warm up several times between takes. Full body and voice work (which requires much space and creates considerable noise) should be done before arriving at the studio.

Below is a series of warm-up exercises that are easily used in the studio and meet the criteria suggested above. Most can be easily done, at least in part, between takes.

EXERCISES FOR RELAXATION

1. *The Roll Down*

This exercise is used by many stage actors and is designed to release tension through the entire spine area. Once spinal tension is released the shoulders drop, articulation becomes clearer, pitch is lower and movement more flowing.

Step A: Stand with feet parallel, about six inches apart.

Step B: Allow the head to drop forward, chin falling onto the chest. Let the weight of the head pull the top of the spin toward the floor. Release one vertebra at a time until the hands are resting or nearly resting on the floor and the body seems suspended by a string from the bottom end of the spine. Knees should be unlocked and bent. (*See illustration 21.*) This exercise is a release, not a stretch. Hang in this position as long as possible. *Allow the breath to flow in and out of the body freely.*

Step C: Beginning at the base of the spine, slowly straighten the spine. Imagine that you are placing one vertebra on top of another until the body is fully erect. The head is the *last* thing to straighten. Be sure to allow the breath to flow in and out freely.

Step D: Repeat the entire exercise. Guard against speed. Each complete sequence will require several minutes or more.

2. *Rotations*

Rotations are designed to relax the individual body parts and to promote the ability to control and isolate tension in particular areas. A rotation is a circular motion of an isolated body part, done continuously and without strain. You can gently and slowly rotate your head, your shoulders, your hands, elbows, upper torso, pelvic area, legs and feet. Try to move only the specific body part. If an area is very tense, you may well hear popping or cracking sounds as it is moved. Be sure to allow the breath to flow freely in and out of the body as you do the rotations. Again, remember the exercise is for release, not for a stretch.

3. *Face and Jaw Relaxation*

   Step A: Closing the eyes, take the fingertips of both hands and place them on the forehead. Make small circles, moving the skin slowly and deeply. Work these circles slowly down around the eyes, down the outside of the nose, out over cheeks, deeply into the top of the jaw hinge. Keep working back in around the lips and chin, then back out along the jawline. Finish with the sides of the neck (avoid the throat itself). Relax with eyes closed and feel the release. Repeat if you have time.

Illustration 21

Step B: Put both hands lightly over your ears, resting the heels of the palms on top of the jaw hinge. Push downward firmly, pressing the hand-heels along the jawline to the point of the chin. Let the mouth hand open as you do this. Repeat several times, until the mouth naturally hangs open without any effort.

Step C: Close the lips and fill the mouth with air. Breathe through the nose and seal the air into the mouth and throat. Imagine you have about fifty cents worth of bubble gum in your mouth and begin to chew the air. Work the large air bubble around in either cheek and through the teeth by the lips. You will get a full stretch of the lower half of the face after about thirty seconds of chewing.

Step D: "The Lion" (a classic Yoga asana for face and breathing). Begin by inhaling slowly and deeply while thrusting the head upward. When you are full of air, push the face forward. Simultaneously stretch and distort the face the following ways: thrust up the eyebrows as high as they go, bug the eyes as large as possible, drop the jaw and open the mouth fully, stick the tongue out all the way. You should look like a cross between a silent scream and the world's largest yawn. Hold this position for a few seconds, then begin to release the breath slowly, gently, in a soft "h" sound from the back of the throat. When the air is gone, relax completely and close your eyes. You should have looked like a slow-motion, silent lion's roar. Repeat two more times, relaxing completely between each one.

Step E: Relax the jaw and shake the face and head back and forth. Blow and exhale breath out the mouth and envision the face as rubber. Stretch every movable muscle on the face and attempt to work things independently of each other—jaw and eyebrows, mouth and forehead.

EXERCISES FOR THE VOICE AND BREATH

All of the exercises listed above for relaxation of the physical body will also serve as exercises for the voice. The series for the face and jaw are particularly critical, even if you are only doing a voice-over. The "roll-down" and "rotations" can be modified as follows:

Exercise 1: As you do the "roll-down" series, let your mouth hang open and the jaw loose. Release the breath on a sound such as "ah" or "o." Allow the breath to flow into the body as you roll up.

Exercise 2: When rotating the head, allow the jaw to hang loose and the mouth to fall open. Emit an "ah" sound during the rotation.

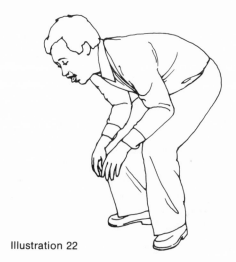

Illustration 22

Exercise 3: Panting improves breath control. Bend over the knees and rest the elbows and forearms on top of the thighs just above the knees (*see illustration 22*). Let the head hang down freely and the jaw hang open. Exhale and empty all the air from your lungs by sharply drawing your belly in and up toward the chest. Release it just enough to let some air come back on an inhale. Contract the stomach inward and upward quickly for exhale, releasing for inhale. The breath should pass easily through nose and mouth. Add sound and vocalize the pant. Each pant should come at about one second intervals, but you must find a rhythm you can maintain. Two or three minutes may be enough to sustain the panting at first, but gradually you may move up to ten minutes or even longer. You will not get dizzy or hyperventilate if you take in and let out the same amount of air constantly.

Exercise 4: Arm swings open the chest area and improve the free flow of the breath. (*See illustration 23*).

    Step A: Stand with your feet flexed and your knees parallel, your arms hanging loosely by your sides.

    Step B: Swing your arms backward and over your head so that they make a complete circle. As your arms swing forward and down, bend your knees so that as the circle is completed your hands almost touch the floor. (You are now crouching.)

    Step C: Your arms swing forward over your head, back and down, completing another circle. As your arms swing forward and over your head, they lift you to your erect starting position.

There should be no stop between Steps B and C. The swinging and bending should be continuous, so that the swinging arms seem to carry the body up and down. Breathing must be coordinated. You should exhale, making the sound "ha" on Step B and inhaling fully on Step C. The chest should feel open and the mouth and jaw should be loose.

EXERCISES FOR FOCUSING CHARACTER AND PERSONALITY

The exercises in Chapter 13 for characterization are particularly helpful in warm-up work. Even if you have carefully prepared your character before coming to the studio, it is always wise to refresh your work immediately before performing. Review your character biography and move about (while dressing or running lines) from your "lead point;" activate your "center" and move through the specific gestures you have created for your character. In other words, put on your character's physical body and try to refresh your decisions about his or her psychology and history. If you are working as a personality, then be sure to review your relationship to the audience and to rehearse the gestures you most want to use, so that they will be comfortable and seem natural.

Below is a chart with a series of questions to answer and tasks that can be performed as part of your warm-up. Some of the questions apply only to characters; others will be helpful for preparation before a news or a talk show. The chart can be used both with carefully rehearsed work and with work that has been quickly prepared in the studio.

WARM-UP CHART

Body

Answer the questions specifically and perform physically the activities suggested. That is, *do* the walk and gestures you will use for the character or emphasize in your personality.

1. Stance: an animal image or an attitude toward people (for example, a monkey or a defensive position)
2. Weight Placement: hips, thighs, chest (see Chapter 13)
3. Lead Point: the point in the body that seems to carry you through space (*e.g.*, nose, chin) (see Chapter 13)
4. Your most interesting physical point: eyes, mouth, shoulders
5. How and why does your body sell this product? Create this character? Portray this image? (*e.g.*, soft, athletic, glamorous)

Illustration 23

6. Three gestures you wish to use: leaning forward to camera lens, folding hands, brushing aside hair

Voice and Breath

1. Pitch: high, low
2. Rate: rapid, slow
3. Rhythm: flowing, staccato
4. Breath: short, shallow, long

Background

1. Age
2. Name
3. Occupation
4. Brief biography: four or five interesting points that you want the audience to know about you, either as a personality or a character
5. Relationship to other performers or characters: either family or social relationship or interrogator, friend, expert
6. Relationship to audience: expert, best friend, peer
7. Primary objective: either the character's scene objectives for the takes being done or, for a personality or a commercial performer; to advise, to reassure, to encourage
8. In commercial work and some talk shows, what is your exact relationship to the product (*e.g.,* "It changed my life," "I use it," "I read it and am happier"

Answering these questions and doing these tasks each time will prevent you from appearing on set only half in character. not comfortable with your personality image or generally "stale."

MAKEUP AND COSTUME

19

Large TV studios with high-budget projects will always have wardrobe and makeup specialists available. However, situations do arise where performers must be able to select their own costumes and do their own makeup. Therefore, it is important for all performers to know at least some fundamental principles about making up and costuming themselves for the camera.

Costumes and makeup are critical to the performer's image in any working situation. In a dramatic situation, the necessity for a specific style of dress is usually indicated and obvious. On talk shows, newscasts or in training tapes, the performer's makeup and costuming must be selected to complement the personality he or she has created. Above all else, care should be taken to select designs that are flattering to the individual face and body. While it is rarely desirable to be "out of fashion," often the latest fashion in clothes or the highest style in makeup are not the most complimentary to the individual performer. Many contemporary fashions are primarily designed to look good on the bodies and faces of professional models.

High fashion also tends to call attention to itself. That is, the clothes or makeup become noticeable and overpower or take attention away from the personality of the performer. Unless you are selling the makeup or the clothes, such attention is not desirable. The best costume and makeup, as a general rule, is that which blends with the performer to create a harmonious whole.

Such a natural effect is somewhat more difficult to achieve in TV or film than on stage or in life. TV lights change colors, color cameras

177

respond to color differently than does the eye, the close-up reveals normally unseen details, the camera lens distorts shape, while the home viewer sees a miniature image with fairly poor resolution. All of these problems make careful consideration of makeup and costuming in TV not only desirable but mandatory for both men and women in any performance situation. Men who must appear on camera are often resistant to applying makeup; ironically, the natural look they seek is lost under TV lights without makeup.

MAKEUP

Today, a performer is most likely to be working with color equipment; it is best to use and/or buy makeup especially formulated for color TV. Such makeup can then, in most cases, be used for black-and-white shooting as well. RCMA Color Process and Max Factor CTV-W or CTV-M (with appropriate shade numbers) are readily available in large cities or can easily be ordered. These professional products will always give better results than will commercial products sold for street makeup. Stage makeup should be avoided as it is generally too heavy for TV work.

Common makeup items that a performer should be able to apply without help are: 1) base, 2) shading, 3) counter-shading, 4) mascara, 5) eyeliner, 6) eye color (shadow), 7) lip color, 8) cheek color and 9) powder. Below are some general principles and suggestions for using these items to achieve a natural look on color cameras. Character makeup, in film or TV, must be left to experts, as stage principles do not work; any drastic changes generally demand latex prosthetic devices. The camera is extremely discerning, and heavy makeup looks like just that—heavy makeup. It is wise, in TV or film, to err on the side of too little makeup rather than to risk applying too much.

1. *Base* should be applied in a thin coat. On pale skins, a shade lighter is acceptable and will even the skin tone for color cameras. Never apply base in thick layers. Be sure to blend it under the collar and onto the neck and to make up the ears. Also, carefully blend the base into the edge of the hair line.
2. *Counter-shading* is a method for lessening shadows. Generally, the only shadows counter-shaded easily are the ones beneath the eyes. In stage makeup or in black-and-white camera makeup, a lighter shade of base makeup will effectively lessen these shadows. However, with color cameras, such a technique will be visible. The lighter shade of base will simply show up as a different color of makeup. Professional TV makeup includes special products for counter-shading that are co-ordinated with the base. Only these products should be used. They must be applied with a brush carefully on the line of the

shadow and then blended at the edges into the base. Never try to completely remove the shadow, as heavy counter-shading will show. Counter-shading the beard area is common in black and white TV. Otherwise a man with a dark beard may appear to have a dirty face. A base several shades lighter than the skin tone can be used for the counter-shading of a beard. In color TV, a well-blended foundation is usually all that is necessary. Most men do not look natural when the beard shadow is completely removed.

3. *Shading* is used to minimize unwanted facial features such as too wide-set eyes or a double chin. Much shading in TV or film will give a performer a "dirty face" appearance. Without experience or the help of a makeup artist, little or no shading should be attempted. The only areas that can be readily shaded, even by a professional, are the frontal bone (just below the eyebrow), the bridge area of the nose, the hollows of the cheeks (very slightly), and the area beneath the chin.

   In color TV work, colors used for shading must not be mixed; instead, a special grayed shading tone should be used. In a black and white system, a shade darker than the base can be used.

4. Cheek color is usually only used on women. It will help to highlight the cheekbones. Apply it only to these bones. A light color is preferred and should be well blended. Dry brush on "blush"; a cream rouge is acceptable so long as it is color coordinated with the foundation.

5. Eye color is used only on women as a highlight. It accents the eyes and should be color coordinated with the costume and eyes. Light shades give the most natural look, but color cameras will tolerate most shades.

6. Eyeliner, like eye color, is generally only used on women, although a man may use it if the upper lid is very heavy and the eyes tend to disappear. It should be brown for the lower lid and black or brown for the upper lid. Remember the purpose is to emphasize the eye, not the line, so apply it thinly right against the lashes. Begin and end where the lashes do. Do not use a liquid liner, as it will not last during a long work day.

7. *Mascara* may be applied in brown or black. While women generally apply it, men should use it only if the eyelashes are very pale. Brush-on mascara is fine and easiest to use. However, the "longer-lash" types should be avoided, as the tiny particles will be shed on the face. If your lashes are too thin, use false eyelashes. Never darken the lower lashes. Use of an eyelash curler is an excellent way to emphasize lashes.

8. *Eyebrows* must look natural. Men generally do not darken their brows but merely brush them to put the hairs in place and to remove foundation or powder that may have collected on the hairs. If a man's brows are very blond and disappear on camera, then a light brown pencil may be used.

   Whenever pencil is used, it should, in most cases, be a shade lighter than the brow. Blondes should never use a color darker than light brown. Black pencil is acceptable *only* when the hair is a dark, pure black. Nothing makes a person look overly made-up so quickly as too dark or too heavily drawn brows.

The pencil must be "feathered" in so that the strokes appear as natural hairs. It is frequently advisable to use two colors of pencil as hair is never a single color. Insofar as possible, stay within the natural brow line. Pencil used above or below the hairs of brow rarely looks natural. Brows should be plucked only if they are extremely heavy or if they grow heavily over the bridge of the nose.

9. *Lipstick* should be selected from a professional makeup line. Many commercial lipsticks contain dyes that change color shortly after being applied. A light color, not too far removed from the color of the inside of the mouth, is desirable for women. The color should of course blend with clothes. Men generally do not use lip color unless the lips are very pale. Occasionally a man's lips are very red, and the foundation needs to be lightly extended onto the lips.

The sequence is usually most successful if done in the following order: a) beard, b) base, c) counter-shading, d) shading, e) cheek color, f) eye color, g) powder, h) eyebrows, i) eyeliner, j) mascara and k) lip color.

COSTUMING

A few specific principles can be followed on costuming.

1. In all TV situations, neither white nor black should ever be worn. Even very pale blues or yellows can present problems. In color work, strong reds are difficult to balance with skin tones.
2. In shows where lavalier microphones are used and concealed, cotton is the preferred material to have next to the microphone. Polyester is particularly problematical because it makes scraping sounds as it passes across these sensitive microphones.
3. It is wise to assume that cameras add pounds to you, and to select clothes that do not. As mentioned earlier, clothes should be appropriate to the individual figure. High fashion clothes are designed for very slender, tall people and may make the average person look ridiculous.
4. Jewelry must be carefully selected. Dangle earrings, for example, often call attention to themselves each time the performer's head moves. Moreover, shiny jewelry creates problems for the cameras.
5. If possible, it is best to wear contact lens rather than glasses.

SUMMARY

In general, performers should select costume and makeup designs that are most appropriate for their bodies and faces. Makeup should be designed for a natural effect and scaled for the close-up. Street makeup techniques are more useful than those of stage makeup. The performer wants the makeup and costume to be a part of his or her whole image and not to stand out or draw excessive attention to itself. Facility with basic makeup skills is important, but complicated makeup and costume techniques should be left to a professional. Any makeup purchased should be professional color TV makeup.

DOING IT BETTER:
Working with the Limitations of TV

Do performers use the methodology discussed in this book; do they have a clear visual media background and understand the tricks that relate to the nature of TV itself; do they have the integrity to develop full characters out of their own experiences? The answer is, of course, no. Most TV performance is haphazard. Actors learn by doing and not necessarily by doing it well.

It *is* possible for a performer to integrate into a performance all of TV's production and technical constraints: the limitations of screen size, aspect ratio and resolution; the demand for appropriately scaled gestures; the illogic of TV blocking. An actor can have both a larger objective—say, to persuade—and a smaller physical task—to get another character to meet your eyes—that together will create a series of in-body gestures that won't move you into your partner's key light or cut off his face, that will flow to a cut.

THE CRUSH OF NECESSITY

Doing it well on TV is never easy. In most productions, everything is geared for economics, for quick and slick results at minimum cost. Decisions get made for the most trivial but pressing reasons. So many people and so much equipment is involved that the odds for real success, real achievement are rarely very high. Things go wrong; compromise is constantly necessary.

TV actors can easily lose sight of the purpose, the objective of their work. Flexibility is constantly demanded, and the adaptable performer adjusts to the production situation. Integrity can be a real liability to the actor under such working conditions. The performer has to have a very strong sense of purpose to stay centered on honest, thoughtful work in the studio or on location. If you have carefully prepared your work, if you generally understand how things are done in production, you stand a much better chance to survive with integrity. Even better, you can adjust to whatever changes develop, without losing sight of the performance you want to create.

For better or for worse, casting to type dominates the broadcast industry and carries over into much non-broadcast work. If you have any success in casting, the easiest and most rewarding path lies in sticking to your type in hustling other jobs. The limitations on your work, however, makes pigeonholing a really deadly process over the long haul. You get so stuck on a few stock gestures and vocal rhythms that you forget you can do anything else. So do casting directors.

Extend your range wherever you can. Read against type, with material that forces you into new approaches, a new delivery. Play with the age and style of your on-camera image. Use the techniques described in Image, Character, Personality and Role to develop a whole new range of performing. Try comedy, broad farce, straight announcing; run through all the commercial formats discussed in Styles of TV Performance. Even if you can't get cast in a totally new kind of role, you will enrich what you already do.

DOING IT BETTER

Television has been dominated by technical necessity and commercial simplification in style. TV is changing, however. More flexible equipment allows less-expensive production, elaborate editing and effects. TV is being used for non-commercial purposes by people who have fewer limitations in background and viewpoint. In the future, actors can reasonably expect to work in creative collaboration with production personnel. Fixed ways of doing things are breaking down, opening up. Actors can be more than talent.

Television is a performing art. Because of its technical demands, actors must be trained and experienced in the particular realities of TV production to use it properly. But besides being skilled at their craft, TV performers need to cultivate their art. They must get a sense of TV's styles, and how they can best manipulate style in their performance. They must decide what TV material reveals, and whether this is something they want to say. They must also reveal something of themselves in anything they perform. Only then will the TV actor be more than a skilled technician.

TV can be art, although it certainly doesn't have to be. The conventional and the cliché dominate commercial broadcast TV, but other possibilities exist and more alternatives develop every day. The TV actor who has a commitment to the potential of the medium will explore these possibilities diligently, will search for new ways to make video performance a valuable expression.

There are experienced professionals who earn a good living doing superficial, unprepared performing that is commercially marketable. And there are professionals who cannot repeat the same gesture or movement twice. The actor who can do more, who plans and creates with the script, who adjusts to the needs of producer and director and other actors, who takes performing as a serious undertaking and who has competently mastered camera techniques is a rare commodity. With training and commitment, however, such actors have as unlimited a future as the TV medium itself.

BIBLIOGRAPHY

Barnouw, Erik. *Tube of Plenty.* New York: Oxford University Press, 1976.

Benedetti, Robert L. *Seeming, Being and Becoming.* New York: Drama Book Specialists, 1976.

Bensinger, Charles. *The Video Guide.* Santa Barbara, California: Video Info Publications.

Broadcasting. Published weekly. 1735 DeSales Street, NW, Washington, D.C. 20036.

Hagen, Uta, with Haskel Frankel. *Respect for Acting.* New York: MacMillan Publishing Company, 1973.

Hawes, William. *The Performer in Mass Media.* New York: Hastings House, Publishers, Inc. 1978.

Head, Sydney A. *Broadcasting in America,* 3rd ed. Boston: Houghton Mifflin, 1976.

Kehoe, Vincent J-R. *The Technique of Film and Television Make-Up for Color and Black & White.* New York: Hastings House, Publishers, Inc., 1969.

Linklater, Kristin. *Freeing the Natural Voice.* New York: Drama Book Specialists, 1976.

Millerson, Gerald. *The Technique of Television Production,* Revised ed. New York: Hastings House, 1974.

Moore, Sonia. *The Stanislavsky System.* New York: Viking Press, 1978.

Pudovkin, V.I. *Film Technique* (includes *Film Acting*). London: Vision Press, Ltd., 1954.

Robinson, Richard. *The Video Primer.* New York: Links Books, 1974.

Televisions, Box 21068, Washington, D.C. 20009. A quarterly covering all aspects of video production and distribution from an independent, non-profit viewpoint.

The Drama Review, vol. 16, no. 1 (T-53), March, 1972. Acting Issue. New York: New York University. School of the Arts.

Variety (East), 154 46th Street, New York, New York.

Zettl, Herbert. *Television Production Handbook,* 3d ed. Belmont, California: Wadsworth Publishing Company, 1977.

INDEX